Latinas

Latinas

Hispanic Women in the United States

Hedda Garza

University of New Mexico Press
Albuquerque

Originally published in 1994 by Franklin Watts
University of New Mexico Press paperback edition 2001

Library of Congress Cataloging-in-Publication Data

Garza, Hedda.
Latinas : Hispanic women in the United States / Hedda Garza ;
foreword by James D. Cockcroft.
p.   cm.
Originally published: New York : Franklin Watts, 1994.
(The Hispanic experience in the Americas).
Includes bibliographical references and index.
ISBN 0-8263-2360-X (pbk.)
1. Hispanic American women.
2. Hispanic American women—History.
I. Title.

E184.S75 G38 2001
305.48'868073—dc21   2001027812

Contents

For my daughter Antonia—
my most beloved Latina.

Foreword

James D. Cockcroft

On August 23, 1995, less than one year after her pioneering work *Latinas* was first published, Hedda Garza suddenly and unexpectedly died. Latinas and others mourned the loss of a powerful voice for human liberation.

But Hedda Garza's voice still rings out, not only in this new publication of *Latinas* but even on television. In January of 2001, cable television's Media One distributed a three-part series featuring a five-person panel discussing Hedda Garza's last book, *Barred from the Bar,* published after her death. The TV series on women in the legal professions started and ended with film clips from her last public speech on "Why We Need a New Women's Movement for the 21st Century."

In my thirteen years of living and working with Hedda Garza, during which time she averaged writing one book a year, we often spoke about how long it might take before new social movements would explode upon the scene despite the low point reached during the economically "lean and mean" years of Reagan, Bush, and Clinton. Hedda liked to say: "Don't worry, new movements will happen, and soon and we'll be there; *¡presente!*" Truer words were never spoken.

Hedda, a working-class intellectual and brilliant researcher whose Watergate Investigation Index (1982) received *Choice* magazine's Outstanding Academic Book Award, spent her entire life protesting social injustices. She was a leading voice in several major political movements. She rarely missed a march to protest the forces of racism, sexism, class oppression, or war, and once she even ran a strong, if losing, campaign for U.S. Senate—as a socialist!

Hedda Garza was extraordinarily proud to be a woman, a Jew, and a New Yorker, who championed the rights of Latina women. After her death, when I was invited by San Francisco State University's Women's Center to speak on this topic, as well as on the Zapatista movement in Chiapas, the sponsors draped a bilingual banner across the student union's main façade describing the talk as "In Memoriam, Hedda Garza." Quite choked up, I found it hard to speak that day. Fortunately, Hedda's works and examples were so much a part of me that I was able to toss aside my prepared notes and spontaneously give the talk she would have given—as if she were speaking "through me." As we enter the twenty-first century, Latinas and Latinos are among the many who are wondering what will become of Hedda Garza's award-winning books, some of which are going out of print. Prominent historian Rodolfo F. Acuña of the Department of Chicana/o Studies at California State University at Northridge has said of Garza's *Latinas:* "there is not another book in the field to compete with the late Hedda Garza's invaluable work." Numerous Latina scholars have written me to ask if there is not a way for this and other books by Hedda Garza to be re-issued for use in their classrooms. Fortunately, the University of New Mexico Press has heard their call, and here is its answer: *Latinas,* like its author *¡presente!*

Acknowledgments

My gratitude to the trailblazing Latina scholars who dug out the hidden history that made my work possible.

Also, my thanks to the reference librarians at Crandall Library, Glens Falls, New York, who cheerfully searched for these sometimes difficult to locate books. And to Elaine Clark, librarian at the New York State Library in Albany, who I know spent many hours at her computer screen digging out the most recent Equal Opportunity Office Census data on Latinas to help a stranger.

A special word of thanks goes to John Selfridge, Vice President and Senior Editor at Franklin Watts, whose intelligence and farsightedness have encouraged me to do my very best.

And last but not least I must express appreciation for Jim Cockcroft, whose support and love kept me going throughout this project.

introduction

Meet the Latinas: Myth and Reality

Call them Latinas, but you will be using a shortcut word for many different groups of women. Some are the descendants of settlers born in the Southwest when it was under Spanish rule, long before the *Mayflower* brought the Pilgrims to New England. Some are Puerto Rican women *(Puertorriqueñas)* and women from other Caribbean and Latin American nations, thousands of whom arrived by ship in the early days of this century. By the 1980s millions of Puerto Ricans, Dominicans, Cubans, Nicaraguans, and other Central Americans and South Americans were living permanently in the United States. At this very moment, some others are making the journey, trekking thousands of miles from Mexico and Central America or risking death in the rapid currents of the Rio Grande or at the hands of thieves along the Mexico-U.S. border.

Some Latinas come alone and others travel with husbands, fathers, children, friends, and family members. Some are educated and some, illiterate; some are old, some young; they represent a rainbow of colors, ideologies, and skills.

Despite the disparity among the cultures of their countries of origin, all Spanish-speaking people since 1980 have been placed under the rubric *Hispanics* by the U.S. Census Bureau. The word *Hispanic* suggests "Spanish," or white Spaniards, the original conquerors of Latin America. Many Latinos, even though they may consider themselves to be "Dominican," "Colombian," or some other nationality, accept the description *Hispanic* because the use of *Hispanic* is required in official matters. Also, many Latinos want to avoid any social bias against non-white persons.[1]

The Census Bureau's use of racial/color/language labels is a very puzzling thing for "Latinos," as many Hispanics prefer to think of themselves (the masculine word ending in *o* embraces either male or *all* Hispanics, while *Latina*, the feminine, refers only to females). The people of these nations, after all, represent a true human rainbow. Latinos call themselves by many names, including "Cuban American," "Mexican American," and so on.[2]

The Latino group is rapidly becoming the largest minority population in the United States. There is every reason to believe that, given present trends, Latinos will outnumber African Americans in the next decade or two.

The 1990 census reported that 75 percent of the 249 million people in the nation was of European origin. Twenty-nine million African Americans made up 12 percent of the population. Hispanics numbered 22.4 million, not counting up to 5 million who may have been missed by census-takers. Nor did this count include 3.5 million Puerto Ricans who live in Puerto Rico but, as U.S. citizens, move freely back and forth to "the mainland." Comprising the largest group (and who are the longest here) of Hispanics were 13.5 million people of Mexican background. Next were the U.S. mainland Puerto Ricans, numbering 2.7 million; Cubans ranked third at 1 million. The other Hispanic groups—Dominicans, El Salvadorans, Nicaraguans—all were clocked in at less than 1 million, but their ranks are rapidly swelling. Only four other groups classified as "ethnic minorities" had populations above 1 million in 1990—1.9 million American Indians and Alaska Natives and 7 million Asian Americans and Pacific Islanders.

Despite the growing numbers of "minorities" (world-wide, of course, whites are a minority, and in the United States they may be outnumbered by nonwhites by the year 2030), the Anglo-Saxon heritage remains unmistakably the most dominant culture and the background of most prominent U.S. economic leaders. Powerful U.S. institutions (banks, industries, the media) are owned by descendants of British settlers. The lion's share of the wealth of the nation is concentrated in the hands of 2 percent of the population, almost all from original "Yankee" Anglo-Saxon backgrounds.

For many years different ethnic groups of Spanish-speaking people in the United States lived apart from each other (Puerto Ricans in New York City; Mexican Americans in California and the Southwest). Today Latinos are often found in the same neighborhoods and on the same job sites. New York City, for example, has become a gathering place for Puerto Ricans, Dominicans, Central Americans, Cubans, and even Mexicans. They quickly find that they have many similarities aside from language.

Unfortunately, one of the similarities is the effects of racism. As a direct result of this virulent disease, many Latinos live in substandard housing in urban slums, receive inferior education and health care, and work at menial low-paying jobs. They have been blamed for everything from state budget deficits to unemployment, drug addiction, and high crime rates.

Latinas have suffered the double oppression of sex-

13

ism and racism. The darker a Latina's skin color, the more racism she faces—making good jobs and social acceptability even more unobtainable.

Many so-called experts have written books and articles "explaining" Latinos' supposed "failure to succeed." Among the undeniable truths the experts offer is the huge obstacle of poverty. Unfortunately, the experts also offer some pernicious myths. One repeated most often is: "The European immigrants made it. Why can't you?" The implication is that something is wrong with the many Hispanics who remain in poverty. We will make every effort to expose this as a lie.

Even more poisonous, however, are generalizations about some "national character" of Latinos, especially the myth of *machismo*. All-encompassing characterizations— labels called *stereotypes*— about entire racial, ethnic, or religious groups are the fuel of prejudice. *Machismo* is in many ways a far more damaging label than the usual epithets mouthed by ordinary racists because it is put forth as a scholarly "finding" by a wide assortment of social scientists, including many Hispanic scholars. This term is applied to men, but in reality Latinas have suffered just as much from the labeling. From the Spanish spoken in Mexico and other countries, some scholars have coined the concept *hembrismo*, after the word for the female gender of a horse or other livestock animal, *hembra*. The description of *machismo* duplicates in almost every detail the usual definition of European patriarchy. A *macho* man is often described as authoritarian, sexist, and domineering. He is always brave and certainly never sheds a tear. As the supreme boss in his family, he operates under a double standard of sexual behavior. He is permitted, encouraged, and even admired for chasing women, but he insists on marrying a pure and virginal girl who must always be faithful.

When the stereotyped version of Spanish origin is described by many authors, further derogatory characteris-

14

tics are added that *continue to fit the behaviors of all patri-archal and chauvinistic men.* These characteristics include "insensitivity, power, violence; indiscriminate sexual conquest of females with the aim of lowering their status." According to some, it leads to an "escape from reality through alcohol and drug use; and fighting and even killing each other for relatively minor reasons."[3]

The opposite side of *machismo,* of course, is *hembrismo* or its variants—the role assigned to women. In English, we would use the words *femininity, female,* or *womanliness.* All of these words have meant different things in different times and places. In the stereotyped version, the *hembra* is docile and submits to male authority, the same definition of a "good woman" in all patriarchal societies!

The truth is that there is no special domineering behavior applicable to Hispanic men only or submissive behavior applicable to Hispanic women only. Sexism exists in all cultures and has diminished in some only under the intense pressure of women's organized social movements. If machismo is a patho-logical condition, then it is a universal mental disorder!

This unfortunate stereotyping has led to what one researcher sums up as the "classic pathological view" of Mexican families developed by American social scientists: "researcher after researcher, without benefit of empirical evidence, continues to depict a *macho*-dominated, authoritarian Mexican-American family." Yet a study of 100 married Chicano couples in Fresno, California, a cross section of the Chicano population, shows that most couples share in the decision making, with the woman mostly responsible for the home sphere and the man for outside institutions—*as in almost all cultures.* Additional research has exposed similar lies and half-truths about Puerto Rican families.[4]

In every nation around the world women have been and still are treated like second-class citizens. They begin to achieve equality only when they fight back. In every country where some element of freedom of speech existed, small numbers of women struggled to change the rules.

Here and there a few men and male-led organizations stepped forward to support these early "feminists." In the American colonies, Thomas Paine spoke out for women's rights, and Quaker men often assisted women who wanted to attend college. In Mexico Ricardo Flores Magón and his Partido Liberal Mexicano (PLM), a party that operated on both sides of the Mexico-U.S. border in the early 1900s, championed the equality of women.[5] But male supporters were few and far between.

No genuine war has been launched against the *machismo/hembrismo* stereotypes. "*Machismo:* Dead or Alive?" is the question posed by a popular, middle-class oriented magazine for Latinos, *Hispanic.* Some of the words of a song sung by The Village People, "*Macho* Man," lead into the article: "Every man wants to be a *macho macho* man . . . he's a king. Call him Mr. Ego." The author of the article informs us that "*machismo* is a Spanish word that roughly translated means he-man-ship, stud-man-ship."[6] The article's answer to its title's question is that this Latino trait is very much alive and well!

Ultimately, stereotypes are best disproved by the true (and often lost or hidden) history of the slandered people. In the following chapters, you will meet the real-world Latinas whose strength, courage, and accomplishments in the face of racism and sexism are the best ammunition against these cruel distortions. Many of them, known and unknown, some long gone and some still contributing, are "heroes" in every sense of the word. There are many more than we have been able to include. Some are your own mothers, grandmothers, and aunts. Most have been left out of history books. In these pages we hope to introduce you to some of them, the unsung, brave, and wonderful Latinas!

1

UNO

The Invisible Women
of the Golden West

*There will be many [English-speaking people]
coming. Choose from these newcomers men and
women who are of your class. Make them your
friends, and they will respond and be your friends.*
— Advice of the old dons
[early Mexican elite in Southwest],
circa 1870[1]

*At every hour of the day and night, my
countrymen ran to me for protection against
the assaults or exactions of these adventurers.
Some times . . . force had to be resorted to.
How could I have done otherwise? Were not
the victims my own countrymen, friends, and
associates? Could I leave them defenseless,
exposed to the assaults of foreigners,
who . . . treated them worse than brutes?*
— Juan Nepumoceno Seguin,
mayor of San Antonio 1840–42.
Forced to flee to Mexico in 1842.[2]

With only a few exceptions, Hollywood's Westerns have presented a fantasyland picture of the settlement of the Southwest and California. Most Americans believe the story that portrays courageous trailblazers and "Indian fighters" like Buffalo Bill or Kit Carson and thousands of sturdy pioneers occupying "empty" lands.

The truth is startlingly different. The vast lands of the Southwest and California were by no means empty. When the Spaniards conquered Mexico in 1519, naming it New Spain, they sent contingents of male scout-explorers to travel across the barren desert lands of northern Mexico. When they crossed the Rio Grande River into the lands that constitute today's Southwest, they encountered peaceful Pueblo Indians, settled on the fertile riverbanks, and nomadic Apaches and Comanches.[3] In the name of bringing Christianity to the "savages," the explorers established fortified Catholic missions for protection against the very Indians they hoped to reeducate.

The newcomers often exterminated the native Americans' buffalo herds and occupied their lands. Without land or food, the Indians were left with the choice of laboring for the conquerors, continuing their futile efforts to drive them back, or starving to death. In New Mexico, the Pueblo Indians decided to work for the Spaniards. After all, these strange men brought not only guns but chickens, pigs, horses, and cattle, as well as tools for farming and mining. The Pueblos soon found themselves the near-slaves of their "benefactors." The Spaniards mixed with the Indian women and a new generation of Spanish-Indian mixed blood *(mestizo)* children were born—future ancestors of some of today's Chicanos.

Many of the Spanish settlers were disreputable types. Although some married, rape was not uncommon. At the Mission San Gabriel in California, for example, soldiers chased the Indian women to their homes, "lassoed women for their lust and killed such males as dared to interfere."[4] The priests, called padres (fathers), pleaded in vain with the Spanish authorities to send only ethical men. Since the men could not be controlled, the next best method was to lock up young women at night until they could be properly married.

As ranches and towns grew up around the missions, the men, called *dons,* were absolute rulers of their wives and children and their Indian laborers. In exchange for giving up their freedom, the Indians were fed, clothed, and "protected."

Except in their roles as submissive daughters or rape victims, women are seldom mentioned in history books about the old Southwest. Recently, scholars have begun to examine church and court records, old diaries and letters, and the writings of travelers and novelists of the period. They are slowly piecing together the true stories of women's lives. Women often turn up as owners of shops and small businesses, farmers, layministers, godmothers, foster mothers, barmaids, servants, midwives, and even doctors. Unfortunately, the male record keepers seldom noted more than the names and the dates of birth and death of women.[5]

The love story of Bentura de Esquibel and Juana Lujan provides us with one of the few precious records of the private lives of men and women who lived almost three hundred years ago.[6] In Santa Fe, New Mexico, eighteen-year-old Bentura de Esquibel worked as a servant in the home of the colonial governor of New Mexico. He became interested in Juana Lujan, the daughter of another servant, Ana Lujan.

Bentura requested permission to court Juana, but neither set of parents approved. Juana's mother thought that Bentura was lazy and would never amount to anything. Bentura's father believed that "Juana Lujan is not Bentura's equal in honor or racial status."[7] Since Bentura later stated that he was a "Spaniard," we can assume that Juana Lujan was darker skinned than her suitor.

As was the custom, Juana was locked into her room

every night. Not to be stopped by doors and walls, Bentura climbed to Juana's attic window under cover of darkness. He seduced her, promised her marriage, and gave her a silver medal of Our Lady of Guadalupe, his *prenda,* or engagement gift. Word of the romance leaked out and the governor decided to separate the lovers by sending Bentura to another parish for a few months. Before he left, Bentura sent a friend with a message of love for Juana, reaffirming his intention to marry her.

The local priest was final arbitrator on the acceptability of all marriages. Before a couple was permitted to announce their wedding date, their padre conducted a detailed investigation, questioning the bride and groom and their witnesses on possible impediments to marriage—religious differences, previous marriages, and even previous promises of marriage. If all was well, the priest would then announce the engagement in church for three consecutive Sundays, inviting anyone present who had information that he had overlooked to contact him.

Several weeks passed; with her lover still gone, Juana discovered that she was pregnant. Then, attending church one Sunday morning in April 1702, Juana heard the priest tell the congregation that Bentura de Esquibel planned to marry Bernardina Rosa Lucero de Godoy. Since there was no way that she could keep her secret, Juana Lujan informed the priest that Bentura had promised to marry her and taken her virginity.

Several witnesses came forward on Juana Lujan's behalf, including the friend who had carried the messages between the lovers and a neighbor lady who had seen Bentura make his midnight climbs. Since Bentura could not deny his relationship with Juana, he challenged her innocence. The law punished only the seduction of a *virgin.*

Juana Lujan emphatically denied her ex-lover's charge that she was "not chaste." She seemed equally furious over Bentura's claim that she was not "Spanish," as was his new love. She then withdrew her appeal, bravely stating her reasons:

> *What kind of a life would I have to endure if you forced him to marry me? And besides, the governor has threatened me, saying that he will stymie my request by whatever means necessary. I am helpless against the sinister violence of such a formidable adversary.*[8]

The marriage between Bentura de Esquibel and Bernardina Lucero took place, but the Church decided that Bentura would have to pay two hundred pesos to Juana, enough to buy three hundred sheep. Presumably she would then be marriageable despite her pregnancy.

The church fathers and state authorities were often at odds over such cases. The padres were most concerned about morality. The governors cared most about family property's passing into the right hands, rather than belonging to the "inferior" children of racially and economically "inappropriate" marriages. One official ruling in 1753 declared that the marriage of "a maiden seduced under promise of marriage [who] is inferior in status . . . would cause greater dishonor to his lineage . . . than the dishonor that would fall on her by remaining seduced."

This pecking order based on race, class, and gender has persisted up to the present. Although the sanctioned and unsanctioned marriages and births produced a racially mixed mestizo population, many of the lighter-skinned descendants of these early people continued to call themselves "Hispanos" or "Spanish Americans," especially in New Mexico. Rodolfo Acuña, the prominent Chicano historian, calls this a "fantasy heritage" aimed at denying that they are from the same stock as oppressed Mexican immigrant workers.[9]

Not long after Juana Lujan's times, settlers were beginning to hear about events thousands of miles to the east that would eventually disrupt their lives. The young United States, born in the Revolution against the British in 1776, boasted a growing population, including a million slaves. As industry mushroomed in the northeast and prosperous plantations blanketed the South, new immigrants began arriving from Europe and the slave trade increased. The young nation was rapidly developing into an economic power.

Always on the lookout for sources of raw materials, new farmlands, and new markets, ambitious industrialists, plantation owners, and merchants feasted their eyes on the territories of Spain. In 1803, the United States negotiated the peaceful purchase of Louisiana from France. That whetted the appetite of national leaders for more territory. In 1818 U.S. military expeditions easily captured Spanish posts in eastern Florida. A subsequent agreement ceded Florida on condition that the United States would keep its hands off Texas.

Hoots of "No way!" greeted this compromise. Texas was too juicy a plum to pass up, people protested, claiming that Texas was part of the Louisiana Purchase. By 1823, when Mexico finally won its independence from Spain, the fragile newborn Mexican government cast nervous eyes toward its northern territories. Anglo-Americans, many of them bringing in contingents of slaves, were moving in every week.

Many of the new settlers were anti-Catholic. Convinced that God viewed their industrious, "democratic" white Protestant stock as superior to all others, they believed they had the God-given right to own all the land, regardless of Mexicans, native Americans, or anyone else who stood in their way. This attitude became officially codified into the doctrine of Manifest Destiny that "justified" U.S. expansionism into other people's lands, including Latin Americans'.

President John Quincy Adams offered Mexico one million dollars for Texas. Mexico refused the insulting offer. In 1829, Mexico abolished slavery and insisted that settlers in the north (Texas) follow suit. The slave owners "obliged." They "freed" their slaves, signing them on as lifetime indentured servants.

The whites had no intention of remaining under the rule of people they considered inferior. When slaves escaped across the river to freedom in Mexico, slaveholders blamed the Mexicans. Mexico barred further U.S. immigration into its north. In vain, President Andrew Jackson upped Adams's offer to five million.

By 1835, thirty thousand rebellious Anglo-American settlers and two thousand contracted slaves were living in Texas, far outnumbering the five thousand Mexicans. Mexico sent General Santa Anna and an army of about six thousand on a five-month march over hundreds of miles of desert to defend its territory against the whites' insurrection. Ill and exhausted, Santa Anna's men staggered into San Antonio, where about 200 Anglos (Spanish word for English) had barricaded themselves into an old mission, the famous Alamo, intent on holding the city.

The story of the Battle of the Alamo has been reenacted in dozens of Hollywood films, most of them never bothering to inform the viewing public that the "freedom-loving defenders" were attempting to steal Mexican lands. After a bloody battle, the better-armed Anglos were defeated by 1,400 Mexican troops.

The Mexican victory was short lived. Shouting the war cry of "Remember the Alamo!," Sam Houston's army of one thousand attacked and captured Santa Anna. In a spirit of revenge, there was a mass slaughter of Mexicans, and Houston was declared president of the Republic of Texas. The Mexicans living in the area had reason to fear him. During the brief war he had made his attitude clear: "The Anglo-Saxon race must pervade the whole southern extremity of this vast continent. . . . The Mexicans are no better than the Indians and I see no reason why we should not . . . take their land."[10]

The United States held Texas in trusteeship until 1845 and then granted Texas statehood, causing Mexico to sever diplomatic relations. On May 13, 1846, Congress declared war, claiming Mexicans had shot American soldiers "on American territory" 150 miles south of the Mexico-Texas border. Congressman Abraham Lincoln challenged the duplicitous American claim, but to no avail.[11]

American troops leveled the major Mexican border city of Matamoros with a barrage of artillery before capturing it. The brutality of the occupying soldiers was so fierce that General Ulysses S. Grant, later a Civil War hero and president of the United States, wrote in a letter to a friend: "Some of the volunteers and about all the Texans seem to think it perfectly right to impose on the people of a conquered City to any extent, and even murder them where the act can be covered by dark. And how much they seem to enjoy acts of violence too!"[12] Years later he admitted, "I had a horror of the Mexican War . . . only I had not moral courage enough to resign."[13] General Winfield Scott added, "murder, robbery, and rape of mothers and daughters in the presence of tied-up males of the families have been common."[14]

Faced with severe financial problems and Indian uprisings, Mexico had little hope of victory. After four months of brutal warfare, North American troops reached and captured Mexico City on September 14, 1847.[15]

With the signing of the Treaty of Guadalupe Hidalgo, on February 2, 1848, Mexico ceded almost half of its territory, the entire Southwest of today, to the United States. Six years later, in 1854, southern Arizona's rich copper deposits were obtained with the Gadsden Purchase. U.S. industrialists now had access to rich natural resources and cheap or cost-free labor—Mexicans and black slaves.

The Treaty of Guadalupe Hidalgo contained provisions that protected the land rights of Mexicans in their lost territories, but who would enforce the agreements? The Mexicans now living under the rule of the United States had one year to decide to stay or leave. The vast majority, about one hundred thousand, remained on their land.

It was difficult for Anglos arriving in the Southwest to understand the treatment of women there. In the East, married women could not own or inherit property. Traditional Hispanic custom and law protected women's property rights and gave them equal inheritance rights with males. Among the elite, women held significant economic power as large property owners. For Anglo men, intermarriage with daughters of the Hispanic wealthy was advantageous. The Mexican fathers who consented to the matches believed that they were gaining status and protection for themselves and their future grandchildren.[16]

Like Texas, California was an economic plum. The Mexican Republic, which possessed California, proclaimed freer trade policies in the mid-1820s. As a result, hundreds of Anglo traders, whalers and trappers moved into the California area. Within a decade, California had become a vital part of the U.S. economy. The busy harbors of the West Coast were filled with clipper ships stopping along their way to and from the ports of Asia.

President Andrew Jackson tried to buy the territory. After Mexico turned down his offer of half a million dollars for all of northern California, Jackson urged Texan leaders to claim California as part of Texas. John C. Frémont was sent west as head of a U.S. Army mapping expedition. During his sojourn in California in early 1846, he learned that a U.S. war with Mexico was being planned. Deciding to get an early start, he raised the American flag high at Hawks Peak, recruited a group of armed supporters, and declared war on Mexico under a Bear Flag symbol. The Bear Flaggers confiscated the

Mexicans' land and stole their cattle and horses. The famous scout Kit Carson led many of these raids. The U.S. Navy secured the harbor at Los Angeles, and the conquest of California was completed months before the Mexican-American War had begun.

The victory in the U.S.-Mexico War in 1848 gave the United States the most valuable asset of all: gold. As early as 1842 the precious metal had been discovered in California. Mexican, Chilean, and Peruvian miners, already familiar with the techniques of gold mining, taught newly arriving Anglos, who made eager students. At first after the United States annexed California, relations were amicable. Laws were printed in both Spanish and English, and Mexican males were given voting rights. Women, of course, had been excluded from voting by the U.S. Constitution.

With so many people digging and panning for gold, many others came to earn money feeding them, selling supplies, or driving muleteams and laboring for successful miners. A small number of Mexican women lived nearby or traveled to the mining camps and worked as cooks and laundresses. Prostitutes, both Anglo and Mexican, came too, as they always had, to army and navy bases and mining camps, wherever there were many men and too few women.

Soon, the rich deposits began to thin out. Bitter Anglos who had failed to find wealth made the "others," the Latinos, scapegoats for their failure. Due to Anglo pressure, the First Foreign Miners Tax was passed in 1849. The Latinos were suddenly not their friends and teachers but "greasers" (derogatory term for Mexicans) to be taxed, lynched, robbed, and thrown off their claims. By 1850, when California became a state, the Latino Californianos in the north had become a hated, powerless minority, outnumbered ten to one.

Later stories of the gold rush days described two types of Mexican women. The first was a group of aristocratic Spanish "ladies," light-skinned Californianas, who had lived in the area before the Mexican war. The others were labeled prostitutes or the "gun molls" of bandits.[17] No mention was made of Latinas who prepared food and scrubbed dirty clothes for the miners.

It is no surprise that the first woman hanged in California was a slim woman in her mid-twenties named Josefa. In Downieville in 1851, a mob lynched her after a mock trial. She had stabbed a drunken Anglo miner who had broken down her door the night before, cursing and calling her a whore. Josefa was living with a Mexican man and expected his baby. Although there was ample evidence to the contrary, the myth would persist for years that Josefa was a prostitute. In keeping with racist stereotyping, she was stripped of her real name and became "Juanita" in accounts of the tragedy, just as all Mexican men were called "Juan."[18]

By 1851, with gold scarce, land became the reason for coming to the Southwest. Almost as rapidly as they had been deprived of their mining claims, Mexicans lost their land. The guarantees of the Treaty of Guadalupe Hidalgo were usually ignored.

Seeing that the courts would back their claims, squatters camped out on Mexican lands, ambushing the owners and burning their crops. Cases of land disputes were conducted in courts in English and usually were decided in favor of wealthy ranchers and railroad owners. Many Mexican landowners sold out rather than allow a costly litigation process to drag on to certain defeat.

By the 1880s, when the building of the railroads was being completed, most Mexicans lived in poverty, working long hours for low pay in the mines, on the rails, and on lands that once had been theirs. They were pushed into segregated *barrios* (neighborhoods), where epidemics raged and many babies died in infancy. Doctors often refused to treat people in these slums. Mothers suffered terribly.

The new landowners quickly learned that land without labor was useless. There were too few native Americans left alive to recruit enough workers from among them. The landowners feared that Mexican workers might be dangerous for all mistreated people pose a real or imagined threat to those who have harmed them. Thus the period of Chinese immigration to California began. In 1851, four thousand Chinese laborers were working on ranches and in mines. By 1870, when government irrigation projects were under way and railroad tracks were being laid at a furious pace, 40,277 Chinese workers had been brought to California as contract laborers, and now outnumbered the Mexicans.

Thousands of unemployed white workers called for the expulsion of the Chinese. The number of beatings and lynchings increased. This time the Chinese were the victims. Nativism and racism swept the Southwest and California as thousands demanded "America for Americans." In 1882, Congress obliged and passed the Chinese Exclusion Act.

After the Civil War, southern cotton plantations moved deeper into Texas. With slavery abolished, thousands of laborers were needed to clear the land and grow and pick the cotton. Displaced Mexican *rancheros* (farmers) and new arrivals from Mexico worked side by side with freed slaves under the hot sun.

The Texas Rangers, formed in 1835, were expanded to police the new social order. They concentrated on controlling the Mexican workers and preventing labor struggles. Racial violence was a daily event. In self defense, so-called social bandits like the famous Juan "Cheno" Cortina became heroes to the Mexican people when they took up arms and conducted raids against the Anglos who had stolen their land. All Mexicans were blamed for these activities, and retaliatory raids by Anglos were fierce. Women were the victims of sex crimes; men were beaten and lynched. When husbands were murdered, wives were left penniless to raise their children.

Some Mexican American women became directly involved in the resistance, as in the El Paso Salt War of 1877. Salt had been discovered by Mexicans about a hundred miles from El Paso. The salt mine was considered community property. A few dollars could be made collecting and selling it. Efforts to take that meager livelihood away from Mexican men and women led to brutal massacres of Mexicans by Texas Rangers and posses. "Rapes, homicides and other crimes" ended the Salt War.[19] Public pressure led to a congressional investigation, but no one was punished and community ownership was canceled.

The greatest resistance to Anglo occupation was in New Mexico, where the majority of Mexicans in the Southwest lived—some sixty thousand. Charles Bent, a prominent Anglo who had married a Mexican woman, spied on his neighbors, complaining about the "sullen reaction of the 'mongrels' to Anglo-American rule."[20] When Bent was killed by a band of guerrilla fighters and there were several similar attacks throughout the territory, the U.S. Army marched in and occupied the area and governed New Mexico until 1851.

In the years following the military occupation, Anglos seized the Mexican and Native American communal land holdings as well as most private land grants. A political machine, the "Santa Fe Ring," took control, pushing out small Mexican farmers and sheepherders. It took bloody range wars to accomplish the thievery. Texans poured in to New Mexico to reinforce the white minority.

The last major battle by New Mexico's sheepherders and farmers took place from 1876–1878, the "Lincoln County War." Hollywood films have depicted the event as an ongoing fight between "sod-busters" and ranchers.

In reality, it became a race war, won by the superior forces of the Anglo ranchers. Even as late as 1887, resistance continued. *Las Gorras Blancas* (White Caps) organized one thousand five hundred fighters and had many supporters. Federal troops were needed to suppress these freedom fighters. But their struggle for a piece of the soil lived on in story and song.[21]

New Mexico's elite self-styled "Hispanos," mostly well-off merchants and landholders, ignored the maltreatment of their fellow Mexicans, intermarried with whites, and used their Anglo connections to send their children to parochial schools or apprenticeships in St. Louis. But because of continued resistance by the masses of Mexican inhabitants, New Mexico was not granted statehood until 1912.

In 1863, mineral-rich Arizona separated from New Mexico and became the Arizona Territory. Anglo investors from the East took over wealthy mine sites developed by Mexican laborers and prospectors in the "mining triangle" of southern Arizona, southwestern New Mexico, and northern Sonora (Mexico). By 1880 the Southern Pacific railroad had reached Tucson, and its lines spread to the mines and river valleys. With mining and agriculture now possible on a large scale, the population mushroomed. As more Anglo women traveled by train to New Mexico and Arizona, there were fewer intermarriages, weakening the alliances between "Hispanos" and Anglos.

In the mines, Mexicans received less than half of what Anglos earned. Race riots became frequent. Often Latinas became the victims of drunken Anglo rioters, who were intent on proving their superiority to Mexican men by raping their wives and daughters.

All over the Southwest, Latinas sought help from their churches when they were under attack. But the Catholic church was near collapse. In Tucson, Arizona, for example, in 1890, one priest was assigned to a thousand Catholics, mostly Mexican, spread over more than seven thousand square miles of desert and mountains. Powerless, the Church cooperated with the elite, discouraged resistance, and urged parishioners to Americanize.

To most Mexicans, the advice was useless. The Anglos did not treat them like equal American citizens. The American settlers who traveled hundreds of miles to steal the Mexicans' lands were called "brave pioneers," but the Mexicans whose land was taken were described as the "dregs of society, so-called Spaniards, a dissolute lot largely of worthless character."[22]

When slandering the Mexicans, the racists differentiated between men and women. The men were "yellow-bellied greasers" but the women were "styled greasers . . . sensual" or "half-breed temptresses."[23] Labeling the women in this way made it easier to seduce and abandon or even rape them.[24]

Little has ever been written about the invisible Mexican American women of the Southwest to contradict the racist stereotypes of them. Few books even mention their existence. The vast majority of Latinas had little or no schooling, and of course could not set down their experiences on paper. A handful of educated daughters of the elite wrote brief memoirs of their lives. But since they regarded themselves as "Spanish," not Mexican, they usually supported their white conquerors.

Nina Otero-Warren was one of the few Latinas from an elite family who seemed to regret the loss of land and Hispanic culture in New Mexico. Born in 1882, she was sent to private schools. She taught school and in 1917 became school superintendent for Santa Fe County, New Mexico. She never forgot her brothers and sisters, the poor Mexicans of the Southwest. During the Great Depression of the 1930s, she joined the Federal Writers Project and wrote: "This southwestern country explored and settled nearly four hundred years ago by a people who loved nature, worshipped God and feared no evil, is still a region of struggles."[25]

A few middle-class women went into business. Eulalia Elías (1788–1860) ran the first major cattle ranch in Arizona. She was admitted to Arizona Women's Hall of Fame in the 1980s.[26] Some of the women became schoolteachers. But the vast majority of Mexican American women worked, like the men, at low-paying, hard-laboring jobs. By the 1880s, many Latinas were working outside of their homes. With so few having even a patch of land to till, work outside the home was necessary for their survival. The close-knit Mexican American families were breaking down, because thousands of unemployed men had to search for laborers' jobs or travel far from home for seasonal work harvesting the crops. Some of the men never returned.

By 1880 in Los Angeles, almost one-fourth of Mexican families were headed by women putting in a double workday—caring for their families and working on outside jobs as well. They were joined by other Mexicans who were flooding into the manual labor markets of the Southwest and California. The women worked as servants in the homes of the rich, as laundresses, and in fruit canneries and packing sheds. Often they took their children with them to help pick the crops, joining their husbands in the farm fields. The walnut industry in Santa Barbara, for example, made millions while the *Mexicanas* and their children who picked the nuts barely survived. Child labor was widespread throughout the Southwest. When child labor laws were finally passed in 1919, agricultural workers were excluded from their provisions.

In the cities, many Latinas took in boarders and did the cooking and washing for them, or they went outside their homes to clean house for single men. While the women toiled, they tried to figure out how to find a better life. News drifted in of *huelgas* (strikes) by the railroad workers and miners. A few Mexican women had left for the more industrialized Midwest, where they found allies willing to help them earn better pay and conditions.

Women in Texas heard about one of their own—Texas-born Lucía González. She had married an Anglo, Albert Parsons, and moved to Chicago. There, Lucy and Albert were struggling to help the cause of *los pobres*, the poor. They were becoming famous as leaders of a dynamic new labor movement taking the country by storm. Maybe there was hope yet!

2
dos

Visible and
Fighting Back

Born in 1853 in Johnson County, Texas, Lucía Eldine
González never discussed her family background except
to say that she was Mexican. Throughout her life, though,
dark-complexioned "Lucy" (as her friends called her)
was often referred to as "that colored woman" by her enemies.

In 1871, when she was living in Austin, Texas, Lucy
fell in love with Albert Parsons, an outspoken newspaper-
man. The young couple married and moved to Chicago.
Even while Lucía and Albert raised two children, they
worked around the clock to better the conditions of working people. America was industrializing at a feverish pace,
and tens of thousands of workers came looking for work
in the Windy City.

Lucy took in sewing to help feed her family and became all too familiar with the hard grinding lives of the
city's garment workers. Since most labor unions refused
to take women into their ranks, Lucía founded the Chicago Working Woman's Union. Housewives were invited
to join, and the platform of the organization called for
wages for housework as well as equal pay for equal work—

demands that would not be heard again until the birth of the women's movement in 1970! Under pressure from the Working Woman's Union, in 1882, the Knights of Labor finally voted to take women into their ranks. Four years later fifty thousand women workers were paying union dues and strengthening the ranks of labor.

There seemed to be no end to Lucy Parson's energy and determination. In 1885, she joined other women in an effort to organize Chicago seamstresses who worked sixteen hours a day for very low wages in basement sweatshops.

Everywhere in the nation, the ordinary workday was a back-breaking twelve to sixteen hours. The eight-hour day was the central demand of workers. Albert became the editor of *Alarm*, a pro-labor newspaper founded in 1884, and in its pages he and Lucy demanded a better life for working people.

Strikes for the eight-hour work day spread. In 1886, half a million workers carried out one thousand four hundred strikes nationwide.[1] A coalition of labor unions called for a national strike on May 1, 1886, if there was still no law establishing an eight-hour day. Chicago, with forty thousand striking workers, became the center of organizing activity. When their demand for a humane workday was ignored, organized labor's first May Day parade took place on May 1, 1886 in cities all over the nation.

In Chicago, May Day was a peaceful, almost festive affair. Lucy walked near the parade's head, holding hands with Albert. Seven-year-old Lulu held her father's hand, while Albert, Jr., age eight, held his mother's. Two days later, police killed four strikers at the McCormick farm machine factory. A protest rally was called for the following evening, May 4, at Haymarket Square.

Lucy and Albert Parsons were meeting at the *Alarm* office with seamstresses seeking advice on unionizing their workplace when a messenger rushed in to tell them they were wanted right away at Haymarket Square to address the rally. Both of them were known as fine orators, and the workers cheered wildly when they arrived. As the rally wound down, Lucy and Albert, children in tow, adjourned with some friends to Zepf's saloon on the corner to tell stories over mugs of beer.

Suddenly, they heard a deafening sound on the street. Rushing outside, they learned that the police, acting against the mayor's orders, had advanced into the square to disperse the crowd. A bomb had exploded, killing one of the policemen, and the Haymarket Riot was in full swing. Police billy clubs and bullets and hurled rocks and stones flew through the smoke-filled air. When the dust settled, ten people were dead and fifty injured.

Albert Parsons and several other union organizers were arrested. Dozens of witnesses testified at his trial that he had been at a table at Zepf's when the bomb exploded, but the antilabor hysteria of the probusiness press dictated the verdict. Found guilty of conspiring to cause the riot, Albert and six others were sentenced to death by hanging. With her husband on death row, Lucy packed her bags, gathered up her two children, and went on a nationwide speaking tour "to save the lives of seven innocent men, one of whom I love dearer than life itself."[2] Her low, melodious voice reached more than two hundred thousand people in sixteen states. As one labor historian put it: "Starting from almost Lucy Parsons alone, a protest movement grew until it became worldwide and included millions."[3]

But no amount of public protest could save Albert Parsons. Before he was taken to the gallows, Lucy and her children tried to get through police lines to have one last word with Albert. Even that was prevented. They were arrested and locked in a cell.

Seven long years later, in 1893, Illinois governor John Peter Altgeld issued an 18,000-word pardon of Albert Parsons and the other Haymarket martyrs. For Lucy González, justice had arrived—too late!

Despite the tragic death of her husband, Lucy continued to travel, lecture, write, and organize. She was one of the founders of International Labor Defense (ILD), an organization that provided legal assistance to workers and political dissidents for decades. For the next half century, Lucy González Parsons was seen in many parts of the country, in mining and lumbering camps, union halls, and city streets, wherever people were struggling for their rights. She led hunger strikes and marches in Chicago and other cities, spending many a night in jail, worrying about her family.

In 1913, the year she turned sixty, Lucy González stood tall and strong on a makeshift speakers' platform at a demonstration of unemployed workers in Los Angeles. The police charged into the peaceful group, killing one worker and injuring several others. Lucy was arrested, but just weeks later she appeared at a demonstration hundreds of miles north in San Francisco, where workers were demanding three dollars for an eight-hour day.

In 1935, when she was well past her eightieth birthday, this amazing woman remained active in the ILD and wrote the story of the Haymarket affair for a labor newspaper. Friends lent Lucy, who was terribly poor, trolley fare so that she could get around from one Chicago demonstration to another. She died in 1942, at the age of ninety, in a fire at her home—a heroine to millions of American workers but left out of most history books.[4]

During Lucy González's organizing days in Chicago there were fewer than a thousand Mexicans there. Their numbers grew to twenty thousand by the 1920s. Relegated to the worst-paying jobs and never considered "Americans," most Mexican immigrants, unlike new arrivals from Europe, yearned to return to Mexico. They listened closely to those bringing news from across the border, or read Spanish language newspapers. They learned that Porfirio Díaz, the president of Mexico from 1876 to 1911, was seizing the public lands called *ejidos* and turning them over to wealthy landowners and foreign companies. Just as small farmers had lost their lands in the Southwest, five million farmers in Mexico were rapidly losing theirs. They became debt peons working for large agribusinesses. In new factories workers earned starvation wages. Díaz arrested union organizers and any other opponents of his dictatorship. Talk of revolution was spreading.

By the turn of the century, the United States was becoming an industrial powerhouse. More labor was needed. Millions of immigrants were recruited, most of them southern and eastern Europeans who settled in the northeast.

Once railroads were built in Mexico, hundreds of thousands of hungry Mexicans took trains to the border and crossed over into the "land of the free." No border guards stopped them. Labor recruiters urged them to come. Growers in the Southwest and California needed the Mexicans to plant, pick, and pack tons of vegetables and fruits to feed the thousands of new workers arriving every day at Ellis Island on crowded boats from Europe. Texas planters were looking for willing Mexicans to stoop and pick acres upon acres of cotton. Greedy looms waited in the textile mills of New England, where young white immigrant women and children slaved day and night. Mexicans were also needed in the deep dark holes of the copper mines to help hack the metal out of the earth for the thousands of miles of electrical wiring that would light up the nation.[5]

At first the leaders of the new union movement signed Mexican workers into membership, but they were only fair-weather friends. As soon as there was an oversupply of labor and workers were laid off, the union leaders scapegoated Mexicans for the hard times and threw them out of the unions. Without the support of other workers, the Mexicans were forced to accept half the wages paid to whites. Worse yet, the union members called them "scabs"—strikebreakers—and the Mexicans lived in fear of violence.

Latinas in the mining towns of the Southwest, dreary places like Clifton, Morenci, and Metcalfe, Arizona, had terribly hard lives. Their husbands left before the sun came up and returned after dark, always exhausted, often angry. They lived in dank shacks rented from the copper companies, without water or electricity, segregated from other "white" immigrants—Slavs, Greeks, and Italians—whose living conditions were only slightly better. Mexican and European women scrubbed clothes in muddy streams, carried heavy buckets of water to be heated over kerosene stoves, and tried to feed their families on next to nothing.

On payday men brought home coupons called scrip instead of real dollars. The only place where the "money" had any value was at the local store—the company store—owned by the same men who ran the mines. Food in town would have been cheaper, but there was no way to buy it with the "funny money." The scrip was never enough to feed a family, so the company stores gave credit, putting most of the workers deeply in debt. If they tried to leave, the sheriff could come and arrest them for running away from their monetary obligations. It was a vicious cycle of misery. If a child was sick, they simply prayed the child would recover, for hospitals and doctors were for better-off people. Most Latinas gave birth every year or two with only a neighborwoman or midwife in attendance. Many died young.

In most of the mining camps, the women lived in fear as well as poverty. Men could die underground, during cave-ins. Mexican men were frequently beaten up by angry Anglo and foreign-born miners. Some were even murdered. From many a shack the sounds of weeping women and children could be heard almost every day of the week. Even young Mexican children faced daily taunts and attacks by children from the "other side" of the mining camp. In town, *No Mexicans Allowed* signs decorated the doorways of shops.

Once in a while someone came from the outside to make life a little more bearable. Such a visitor was Teresa Urrea, who came to Clifton, Arizona with her father in 1897. To the Mexicans on both sides of the border she became known as the Saint of Cabora.

Urrea was born October 15, 1873, in the state of Sinaloa, Mexico. She was the illegitimate daughter of a poor Yaqui Indian girl, seduced by Don Tomás Urrea, a ranch owner. When Teresa was fifteen, she moved to her father's ranch in Cabora and learned the healing arts from a woman servant. Not long after her arrival at the ranch, Teresa lapsed into a three-month coma. When she regained consciousness, she believed the Virgin Mary had granted her the power to cure the sick.

The Indians living in the area rushed to receive her gentle herbal treatments. When many of them recovered from their illnesses, Teresa's reputation grew. Her support for their struggles against the poor treatment they received from the Díaz government and the Catholic church made her even more popular. The Church denounced her as a heretic. When Díaz ordered his troops to arrest her, the Yaqui Indians ambushed Díaz's soldiers to protect their beloved "Saint Teresa." It was the beginning of the Tomochic War, or Revolt of the Yaquis, and Teresa became a symbol of Yaqui resistance. As they went into battle, the Indians shouted "Viva la Santa de Cabora!" (long live the Saint of Cabora).

In 1892, Díaz exiled Teresa and her father from Mexico. When the townspeople in the border town of Nogales, Arizona, heard they were arriving, they prepared a furnished house for them. In 1896 when a small group of her Yaqui followers attacked the customs house at the border, Teresa was blamed. According to the *New York Times* of August 14, 1896, the Indians raided to seize the "arms, ammunition, and money in the Customs House . . . to start for the City of Mexico to overthrow the Díaz government." About a thousand Yaquis many miles away from the border rose up in sympathy with the raid. Teresa issued a statement denying her involvement, but Díaz successfully pressured the U.S. government to remove her from the border area.

Don Tomás Urrea and his famous daughter moved several times, finally arriving in Clifton, Arizona in 1897. Don Tomás married, and his new wife's home became headquarters for the main revolutionary organization fighting Díaz, the PLM (Mexican Liberal Party). In the poor mining town, Teresa brought comfort to sick miners and their wives and children. Teresa went on a "curing crusade" across the United States, sponsored by an exploitative and fraudulent medical company. In the spring of 1904, Teresa, who had been married twice, returned to Clifton. Her father had died during her absence. With savings from her tour, she built a large house that served as a hospital for the sick and wounded.

In a flood in December 1905, Teresa Urrea spent long hours waist deep in cold water helping to rescue people. Teresa was already infected with tuberculosis, and this exposure was the last straw. She died a few weeks later at the age of thirty-three. Hundreds of Mexicans joined the funeral procession to the cemetery, mourning the passing of one of the few who had cared about them.[6]

Teresa Urrea's hospital had helped make life a little easier for the miners' families, as did their own organizations, the *mutualistas*. These early cooperative self-help societies existed in cities throughout the United States among workers from many different countries. For a few difficult-to-spare cents each week, doctors' bills, funeral expenses, and other emergencies were covered. The *mutualistas* became almost "family" to most Mexicans, although the groups had little real political power. Men like Abraham Salcido, a PLM leader, often helped organize *mutualista* groups. Even more important, PLM members in the mining camps tried to convince the white foreign-born workers to unite with the Mexicans to improve work conditions.

By 1903, there were signs that they were achieving this all-important unity. Many of the women, European immigrants and Mexicans, urged their husbands to join together. It was obvious that all of them were suffering. Word reached the camps from faraway places that when people banded together in common cause, they had a chance of winning some victories.

Eight-hour-day laws had been proposed in several states and passed in a few. Miners' wives learned that even Arizona's legislature, pressured by earlier mine strikes, had passed an eight-hour workday law. The women hoped this would lead to overtime pay and a little more food on the table, and maybe even a piece of chicken on Sunday. But it turned out the Arizona law excluded "foreigners"— which referred to just about all of the miners, Mexicans and European immigrants alike!

When mine company owners refused to concede to the workers' demands for the eight-hour day, fair prices at the company stores, life insurance, and other benefits, one thousand six hundred copper miners in the Clifton-Metcalf-Morenci area walked off the job. Most were Mexicans, but European immigrants struck too. For the women, it was a fearful situation. If the strike went on too long, they would be dreaming not of special Sunday dinners but of any food at all on the table. The company stores refused to give credit to women whose husbands were marching down the muddy streets yelling "Huelga!" (strike). Armed Arizona Rangers waited at the bottom of the road, blocking passage to the mine.

It had been raining most of the time during the six days of the strike. The banks of the Gila River were already under water and the rain continued to pour down. As more strikers from Metcalf marched down the canyon, a huge wave of water crashed over them and on into town. On the muddy hills and along the river banks, some of the shacks collapsed under tons of mud. Screams were heard from all directions. When the river receded, fifty people lay dead, either drowned or buried in the rubble of their shantytowns. Women wept over the battered corpses of their children.

The disaster seemed to strengthen the resolve of the miners and their families. The following day, armed miners seized some of the companies' ore-processing facilities. Federal troops and national guardsmen were sent in, and the miners, completely outnumbered, continued to fight. Abraham Salcido and other strike leaders were arrested and imprisoned.

The courage of the Mexican miners had a profound effect on many other working people. The American Federation of Labor (AFL) continued to exclude them, but the Western Federation of Miners (WFM) enthusiastically welcomed them. In 1905, WFM delegates attended a convention to organize "One Big Union" for all workers—named the International Workers of the World (IWW), but known far and wide as the "Wobblies." Lucy González Parsons was present, making it clear that women, Mexican migrant workers, and all nationalities and races, as well as the unemployed, were to be full and equal members of the new union. The founders dreamed of a far-off day when working people would govern, in what they called an "industrial democracy."[7]

About five years later the AFL, losing members to the IWW, started to recognize unions of Mexican immigrant workers as "affiliates." The strengthened union movement began to win a few strikes, but as usual when the economy tightened, the fragile unity between immigrant groups was often destroyed.

After serving his jail time, Abraham Salcido was deported back to Mexico. Once again he worked with fellow PLM leaders. They traveled all over to the mining towns of Mexico and the United States, helping the workers organize and raising money for arms with which to overthrow Díaz. PLM leader Ricardo Flores Magón had founded the popular newspaper *Regeneración* (Regeneration). Thirty thousand people on both sides of the border read it avidly.[8]

The PLM had advocated the rights of women from its earliest days and now invited women to join as full-fledged members. In his essay "A la Mujer" (to the women), appearing in *Regeneración* on September 24, 1910, Flores Magón wrote:

> . . . *women work more than men, they are paid less, and misery, mistreatment and insult are today as yesterday the bitter harvest for a whole existence of sacrifice. . . . Bondage does not recognize sex; the infamy that degrades men equally degrades you.*[9]

Dozens of women were active in the PLM and other anti-Díaz organizations. In no way did they resemble the stereotyped portrait of weak and submissive Latinas, dominated by macho men.

Juana Belén Gutiérrez de Mendoza, only one of many exemplary women, was born in Durango, Mexico in 1875. She managed to become a teacher, one of the few professions open to women in Mexico and the United States. Concerned with poor Indian children and working people, she taught a miner, Cirilo Mendoza, how to read and write, and they fell in love. In 1901 she founded her own newspaper, *Vésper*. In its pages she fought for the cause of the miners and attacked the reactionary Catholic church. The Díaz dictatorship frequently shut down her newspaper and jailed her. Behind bars she often had the company of other anti-Díaz women—Dolores Jiménez y Muro, Inés Malvaéz, and Elisa Acuña y Rossetti.

Ordered into exile, Juana traveled with Elisa Acuña to San Antonio, Texas, intent on continuing to publish her newspaper. With Elisa and Dolores Jiménez y Muro she formed a feminist group, Hijas de Cuauhtémoc. The organization worked to improve the economic and intellectual status of women. Later, both Juana and Elisa returned to Mexico and joined the revolutionary army of peasant leader Emiliano Zapata. Juana commanded troops and achieved the rank of colonel.[10]

PLM spokesperson Sara Estela Ramírez was well known on the U.S. side of the border. Born in Mexico in 1881, she attended a teachers college in Saltillo, Mexico and at the age of seventeen moved to Laredo, Texas. Earning her living as a Spanish teacher, she was known to thousands of *Tejanos* as a labor organizer, human rights activist, and poet. In her many speeches, she encouraged women to be politically active. She died in 1910 at the age of twenty-nine, but her poetry still makes sense to many people. "The worker is the arm, the heart of the world," is a line from one of her poems.[11]

The same year that Ramírez died, the PLM strengthened its Los Angeles office. The *Los Angeles Times* launched a campaign against the organization, publishing cartoons and editorials ridiculing PLM members, but thousands of Mexican men and women were more impressed by the commitment of the PLM to the rights of all. PLM words were matched by action. It had conducted historic strikes and revolts throughout Mexico in 1906 and 1908. When the Mexican Revolution broke out in 1910–1911, PLM was a pivotal military force in the overthrow of Díaz. The presence of women was so apparent that the *New York Times* of May 10, 1911 commented that "women have taken a spectacular part in the revolution."

In recent years, feminist writers have criticized the PLM, pointing out that some of the leaders had less than favorable positions on the role of women. "For all their radicalism the PLM male leaders did not move entirely beyond their traditional views of women," one author complains.[12] This, of course, should not surprise anyone.

There undoubtedly was a minority of men within the organization who believed that Flores Magón had gone too far and that women in the organization should limit their activities to nurturing roles. A closer examination of the role of women in the United States during that same period, however, demonstrates that the PLM was decades ahead of its time.

Nevertheless, the myth persists that American feminism eventually influenced Mexican women.[13] Nothing could be further from the truth. Generations of women seeking equality in the United States gave little thought to their Mexican "sisters" in the Southwest. In fact, to gain the vote they eventually turned against them!

During the famous Women's Rights Convention in Seneca Falls, New York, in 1848, when three hundred people met to call for equality for both sexes, the U.S.-Mexico War was raging. While a mostly middle-class group in Seneca Falls discussed women's oppression, Mexican women in Texas, California, New Mexico, and Arizona were living in a state of dread, surrounded by Anglo violence. The delegates voted to concentrate on winning the right to vote.

After the Civil War, with women still kept away from the ballot box, some suffragists implemented new strategies that made enemies of black, Latina, and immigrant women. President William Howard Taft told leaders of the National American Woman Suffrage Association (NAWSA) that he feared "undesirable elements," a code word for immigrants, "might have a hand in determining political leaders." In order to allay such fears, respected NAWSA leader Elizabeth Cady Stanton called for literacy tests and educational qualifications as requirements for voting. In public statements NAWSA criticized the right of illiterate male immigrants to vote and looked forward to the potential political power of professional women. Elizabeth Stanton's daughter, Harriet Stanton Blatch, wrote an open letter to her mother protesting this approach, but she was in a distinct minority within NAWSA.

The feminists' decision to tie voting rights to literacy tests was formalized in 1903. It was small wonder that woman labor leaders, white, black, and Chicana, persons like Lucy González Parsons and organizations such as the Hijas de Cuauhtémoc, stayed away from NAWSA. Only a few Latinas like Nina Otero-Warren, the school superintendent for Santa Fe County, joined the suffrage movement. Otero-Warren became a leader of New Mexico's Congressional Union, a chapter of NAWSA.[14]

In the same spirit of disgraceful compromise, NAWSA bent to the pressures of the Southern-based Woman Suffrage Conference. The Southern women wanted voting rights on a state-by-state basis so that black women could be deprived of the vote. NAWSA leaders gave in to the Southern women, although women in the organization, some from families that had fought against slavery, protested. Forgotten was the early history of the movement when the suffragists had been abolitionists. Debates divided the movement sharply. When the women's suffrage amendment was passed in 1919, the women's movement went into a fifty-year state of dormancy.[15]

Black women, Latinas, and many white immigrant women were effectively barred from voting by poll taxes, fear of deportations, and literacy tests.

While suffragists were busy agitating for the vote, Mexican American women in the plazas of Mexican neighborhoods in Los Angeles, Tucson, and San Antonio, were listening to men and women of the PLM talk about the rights of all workers, including women. In 1911, when the PLM invaded and briefly ruled Baja California, PLM soldiers Margarita Ortega and her daughter Rosaura Gotari acted as messengers and gun runners across enemy lines. Gotari was killed by Mexican soldiers. Two years later, Ortega was captured, tortured, and executed.

María Talavera, Ricardo Flores Magón's companion

(the PLM did not believe in the legal marriages performed by the Church and government they opposed), was frequently arrested and imprisoned because of her association with Flores Magón. The *Los Angeles Times* described her as "a brilliant and bold woman anarchist who dared more than any of the men."[16]

After the Mexican Revolution broke out, more Mexican families fled the violence and crossed the border looking for peace. But jobs grew scarcer, especially during the 1913 recession, and the newly arriving Mexicans encountered a different sort of violence. The newspapers played up so-called plots by Mexican revolutionaries, stirring up anti-Mexican sentiment. Mexicans were scapegoated for the recession, and the number of incidents of anti-Mexican violence rose sharply.

The worst episode of all occurred in the coal mining town of Ludlow, Colorado on April 20, 1914. It would forever be called "the Ludlow Massacre."

Ten years earlier, Mexican miners had been brought into the area to break the United Mine Workers' union. Instead, they joined the union. Now, in 1913, about twelve thousand workers were trying to avoid a strike. They wanted the mine companies, especially the Colorado Fuel and Iron Company owned by millionaire John D. Rockefeller, to simply obey Colorado laws covering work hours, safety measures in the dangerous mines, and cash wages rather than the hated scrip. Instead, Rockefeller and other owners stockpiled weapons and hired more guards.

The strike started on September 22, 1913, a day of hard winds and driving rain. As soon as the men left for the picket lines, women saw armed guards approaching their shacks. At each doorway the guards gave the orders: clear out or be cleared out! With guns pointed at them and their terrified children, the women hastily gathered their few possessions—ragged clothing, dented pots, and chipped dishes. Some of the guards grew tired of waiting and tossed occupants and their possessions out into the mud.

The union immediately set up tent colonies in Ludlow and nearby areas to shelter the evicted families. Through the harsh long winter of 1913–1914, the strikers and their families barely survived. When the word of their plight spread, contributions of food and warm clothing came in from union families in other parts of the Southwest. If not for that solidarity, the families might never have survived the winter.

When the company rustled up some poverty-stricken workers to break the strike, clashes broke out between the strikers and the company's armed guards and local deputy sheriffs. At the end of October 1913, the governor of Colorado dispatched National Guard troops to the area. They did little to stop the harassment of the workers by the company's hired thugs. In fact, one group of guards mounted a machine gun on a car and sprayed bullets in the direction of the tents every time it drove past.

The occupants of the tent colony lived in a state of terror. Mothers taught their children to hide under their cots. Some of the fathers dug deep pits, like bomb shelters, to protect their families. The miners stationed a ring of their own guards in a circle outside the tent area. Meanwhile, union leaders tried unsuccessfully to negotiate with the mine owners.

On the morning of April 20, 1914, the largest tent colony was sprayed with machine-gun fire. Women gathered up their children and raced for their underground shelters or cowered under their cots. That evening, they fed their children what little there was and tried to calm them. Suddenly, as they dozed fitfully, smoke filled their tents and shelters. The terrifying shout of "Fire!" rang through the area. The militiamen had thrown flaming torches at the ragged tents. Women with their clothing on fire, clutching tiny babies, raced from the tents, searching for hiding places. When daybreak came over the smoking ruins, a body count was taken. Twenty-six people had died from burns and suffocation in the fiery blazes. In one of the underground shelters, the charred bodies of two Mexican women and eleven children were found.

In the days that followed, miners poured in from New Mexico to protest the massacre. Three union men were murdered while they were held prisoner by the militia. President Woodrow Wilson dispatched federal troops to calm things down and offered to help find a solution. Company officials refused his offer, despite the death of forty-six more men, including company guards.

After almost a year of near starvation, the striking miners drifted away from the area. The mine owners had brought in nonunion men, and the exhausted and grieving union families were powerless to stop them.

Protest meetings were held all over the country, and there were regular picket lines in front of John D. Rockefeller's offices in New York, Chicago, and San Francisco. Prominent people from all walks of life joined in the outcry. A Denver judge accompanied a group of miners' wives on a cross-country tour to spread the story of the terrible massacre.

A year passed before President Wilson sent an investigation commission to the area. Its report confirmed the testimony of the miners and their wives, but by then it was too late: Tiny graves held the bodies of the miners' innocent children, and the strike had been lost.

To counter the bad publicity, the Rockefeller family launched a public relations campaign to change its image and offered to allow company-controlled unions in the Colorado mines. Here and there, a few strikes were won and a few pennies more were brought home, but Sunday chicken dinners remained a longed-for dream, something strictly for *los ricos* (the rich).

While mining families struggled in the Southwest, millions of Americans ate vegetables and fruits that had been shipped in new refrigerator cars. They wore clothing made of cotton from thousands of acres of cotton fields in Texas and the South and of wool sheared from sheep grazing in the Southwest. Few even thought about the toiling farm workers, mostly Mexicans but also Japanese and Filipinos, who were brought to the United States as virtual contract laborers. A trade magazine of the California growers noted in 1907 that Mexicans were "plentiful, generally peaceable, and are satisfied with very low social conditions."[17]

Those "low social conditions" impacted hard on Latinas working in the fields. Their "homes" were worse than the shacks of the miners. Mexican families lived in huts or simply slept and cooked on the ground near the fields, packing sheds, and canneries where they worked. They occasionally walked off the job, demanding better conditions, but it was easy for employers to round up another crew across the border and expel the "troublemakers," creating a "revolving door" of importation-deportation of Mexicans.[18]

During the 1910s, all Mexicans became suspect, and beatings and shootings became ordinary events. Mexican American leaders, most of them middle class, met for El Primer Congreso Mexicanista (the First Mexican Congress) on September 11, 1911 to discuss the worsening situation. The gathering created La Liga Femenil Mexicanista (Mexican Women's League). Most of the women were schoolteachers, and they heard daily about the violence against Mexicans from their pupils.

By 1914, World War I, the "war to end all wars," raged in Europe. President Wilson was determined to keep Americans out of the conflict, but the United States supported the cause of England, France, and Russia—the Allies—against the Germans. Huge profits were to be made selling war supplies to the Allies. The need for workers to produce steel, copper, and munitions increased enormously.

At first miners and farm workers hoped that their conditions would improve as production in the mines doubled and tripled. But instead a much wider reign of terror began, and fear stalked the border areas. It would go down in history as the "Brown Scare." Mexican and Mexican American labor unionists were called German spies as America's entry into the war seemed inevitable.

Once again Mexican families waited as dusk approached, fearful that a knock on the door would mean the announcement of another death. By 1917, thirty-five thousand U.S. soldiers were stationed at the border. In an article in a news magazine that year, the writer commented that, "The killing of Mexicans . . . in these last four years is almost incredible. . . . There is no penalty for killing, no jury along the border would ever convict a white man for shooting a Mexican."[19]

There was even talk of rounding up all Mexicans and Mexican Americans and placing them in camps. But it was cheaper to ship Mexicans across the border than to house them in camps. One of the tragedies of the Brown Scare period took place during the summer of 1917. In Bisbee, Arizona, during a miners' strike against Phelps Dodge, the local sheriff sent his men and members of the Bisbee Loyalty League, the town's anti-immigrant organization, to occupy the telephone and telegraph offices so that no one could call for help. Over a thousand Mexicans, both citizens and noncitizens, were pulled out of their homes at gunpoint, loaded into boxcars, and shipped like cattle to Columbus, New Mexico. In Columbus, another group of "patriots" dumped them in the sweltering desert without water or food. From there, they staggered across the border to Mexico. When the news spread, anti-American protests took place in many Mexican cities. Months later a government investigation led to the indictment of the president of the mining company, but he was never put on trial.

The previous April, the United States had entered the war, and in May Congress passed the Selective Service Act, making military service obligatory for young men. Mexican Americans and Mexicans with their first naturalization papers were eligible for the draft, but *all* Mexicans were required to register. Some Mexican citizens were mistakenly drafted and marched off to fight in Europe.[20] Facing violence at the border and the threat of being forced to fight in a foreign war, ten thousand Mexicans went home, many of them never to return. In Mexico, the Revolution had calmed down, and at least there would be no racism.

As men in Europe were drafted into their own armies and as Americans joined them on the bloody battlefields, the supply of both U.S.-born and immigrant labor dried up. At the same time, industry and agriculture needed thousands of additional workers. In 1914, over a million Europeans came to the United States. Three years later, fewer than 300,000 arrived.

As the labor supply dwindled, employers once again wanted Mexican workers. Taxes at the border were suspended, and Mexicans were excluded from the literacy provisions of new immigration laws. The hope of jobs that had never before been open to Mexicans, in Texas oil fields, Chicago steel mills, Kansas City meat packing plants, and the vast agricultural fields of California, overcame fears of new "Brown Scares." Mexicans rushed over the border and others migrated from the Southwest and California and Texas farms to line up for jobs in the midwestern cities. Almost 700,000 Mexicans and their families lived in the United States by 1920.

In time for the arrival of thousands of new workers from Mexico and all over the nation, the 1917 Espionage Act and 1918 Sedition Act were passed by Congress. Under those laws, anyone who had not yet attained citizenship could be deported as an undesirable alien. During the Palmer Raids, named after Attorney General A. Mitchell Palmer, armed men from the Justice Department burst into the homes of more than ten thousand union members and labor organizers, European and Latino, and expelled them from the United States. A few congressmen protested, but if they were too loud in their complaints, they too could be labeled Communist or Socialist.

The IWW, the union that had attempted to help the lowest paid workers, including Mexican agricultural migrants who accounted for half its dues, became a favorite target of the authorities. IWW leaders who were not citizens were expelled from the country, but that was not the end of it. The remaining leaders who were U.S. citizens were arrested, tried under "conspiracy" laws and sent to jail for many years. To make sure that the IWW would be permanently crippled, a fine of two and a half million dollars was imposed, bankrupting the union.

In the cities of North America, Mexicans found few friends and terrible conditions. Most Mexicans, as well as the twenty-five thousand or so Puerto Ricans and other Latinos, were hired to perform the most menial tasks in the factories, with little chance for advancement. Living conditions in segregated slum areas were wretched.

Latinos migrating from the Southwest knew about unions, but sometimes crews of workers coming directly from Mexico were brought to steel plants in Chicago when workers were on strike. The Mexicans were placed under guard while they worked and threatened by angry union pickets. But the divide-and-conquer method succeeded only briefly. Mexican union members were able to explain the situation to the new arrivals, enrolling many of them in the union or making sure they left the area.

During the 1910s and 1920s, as prices rose sky high, Latinas tried to scratch together extra money. Only a few jobs for women were available and often there were little children at home who needed their mothers. Like millions of other women of immigrant families all over the country, Latinas took in boarders. The women cooked all the meals for the boarders and their own families and did their washing and ironing and cleaning chores as well. The burden of so many hours of housework, frequent pregnancies, and little or no medical attention turned most Latinas into old women at a young age. Many succumbed to diseases like tuberculosis, which swept through the crowded neighborhoods.

Jobs available outside the home were always at the bottom of the ladder. In El Paso, Texas, women scrubbed over steaming tubs in laundries and bent over sewing machines in crowded garment factories. In 1919, a state commission found that Mexican women were "the lowest paid and most vulnerable workers in the city."[21] They earned less than half the wages of Anglo women, who in turn were paid far less than men. When a Mexican woman managed to land a job as a clerk or in a department store, she almost always worked in the basement stockroom or at the rear of the office, out of sight.

Only a tiny group of educated Mexicans were able to land white collar jobs or become professionals. In Los Angeles in 1900 there were less than three percent in those categories, and twenty years later the number had been cut in half. By 1920, when Los Angeles had the highest Mexican population of any city in the United States, almost 90 percent of Mexicans worked as unskilled laborers, while almost half of the Anglos who had been in that category had moved up to better jobs.

Some professionals tried to improve the situation. Beatriz Blanca de Hinojosa wrote for San Antonio's Spanish-language daily *La Prensa*. She covered women's issues and pressed for women's equality. Another Latina newspaperwoman, María Luisa Garza, attended the 1922 Pan American Women's conference in Baltimore and founded a small feminist group.

The economic misery of most Mexicans seriously affected the health of their children. In Los Angeles in the 1920s, more than twice as many Mexican babies as Anglo babies died in infancy. Tuberculosis rates for Mexicans were far higher than for other groups. Mexican and Mexican American mothers wanted something better for their children. However little schooling they themselves had received, the mothers fought for their children's education.

In 1910, for example, in San Angelo, Texas, Mexicans were about one-tenth of the population of ten thousand. After new school buildings were constructed to replace the shabby and dangerous old buildings, mothers taking their children to the first day of class were told that the two hundred Mexican children must continue to learn in the old school. The mothers got together and decided to keep their children at home. State aid to education, then as today, was based on a head count of the students. The Mexican parents announced that until they received the *benefits* of those payments, their children would go uncounted. The school board still refused to allow the children into the new school; when they appeared, guards blocked the entrance. The board insisted that admitting the children "would . . . demoralize the entire system and they will not under any pressure consider such a thing."[22]

Some of the parents sent their children to a Catholic school. But with more American-born Catholics coming to the areas and joining the church, the Catholic Mexican children were placed in a separate "Mexican room." The Protestant Presbyterian church set up a *separate* mission school for Mexican children in 1912. Since the church schools charged tuition and were also segregated, the Mexican parents finally gave up and sent their children to the *free* segregated public schools in 1915.

For most Latinas in the 1920s, the eight-hour day and a living wage remained only a dream. By the late 1920s, many efforts were being made to improve the situation. With the IWW dismantled, Mexican *mutualistas* founded new groups among the farm workers. There were several agricultural strikes, most of them broken through the use of the border's "revolving door." Middle-class Latinos organized the male-only, citizens-only United Latin American Citizens (LULAC) in Corpus Christi,

Texas, in 1929, to fight for the civil rights of Mexican Americans (see chapter 3).[23]

No one could have predicted that in a matter of months a devastating economic depression would sweep over the whole country and most of the world. All people would suffer, but the "invisible" Latino laborers who fed and clothed the nation would be among the worst victims of the 1930's Great Depression. Dynamic women, barred from LULAC membership, would play a leading role in new struggles just over the horizon.

3
tres

Through
Hunger,
War and
Witch-Hunt

In 1929, the bottom dropped out of the economy when the stock market crashed in October. By spring, when unemployed people went to the bank to draw out their savings, they were told that their banks were closed—five thousand of them.

More than half the nation's Latinos were living in cities by then. They were among the hardest hit—like African Americans, the first to be fired. The sidewalks of the cities soon filled with homeless people, their clothing and furniture dumped on the street when they couldn't meet the rent. Long lines of hungry people waited desperately for bowls of watery soup and stingy pieces of bread handed out by charity organizations. In Chicago, five hundred school children, "most with haggard faces and in tattered clothes, paraded through Chicago's downtown sec-

58

tion to the Board of Education offices to demand that the school system provide them with food."[1]

People fought back everywhere. What angered them most was that apartments stood empty while people slept in the streets; warehouses were filled with food and people had nothing to eat. In several cities when the police put furniture out on the street, crowds carried it back in when the authorities left. In some farm towns, men stormed warehouses and "looted" crates of food. Police reserves were called in to violently disperse them.

World War I veterans were especially angry. They had done their duty, they felt, and now they were being ignored. After the war they had received bonus certificates, redeemable many years later. But they needed the money immediately to feed their children. More than twenty thousand men and their families, from dozens of ethnic and racial backgrounds, converged on Washington in the spring of 1932. They camped in makeshift shacks across the Potomac River in view of the White House. President Herbert Hoover ordered future World War II heroes General Douglas MacArthur and his aides, Dwight D. Eisenhower and George S. Patton, to drive them away. Tear gas was pumped over the area and soldiers burned down the encampment as people fled the fumes. For a few, it brought back memories of the Ludlow Massacre.

Latinos were again scapegoated for economic hard times. The "eugenics" movement, popular in the 1920s, reawakened with new vigor. Women like Margaret Sanger, a champion of birth control a decade earlier, spoke out for sterilization of the poor and unemployed. Many Latinas were tricked into sterilization procedures when they visited clinics and hospitals.[2]

During the first months of the depression, debates raged in Congress over legislation that would "get rid of" the Mexicans. The Harris bill proposed to slash legal immigration of Mexicans from fifty-eight thousand to a mere one thousand nine hundred. Representatives of agricultural and industrial interests opposed the idea. They knew wages could be kept down if there were large numbers of unemployed workers, including Mexicans, competing for the same jobs. One of these "allies" testified that "The Mexican is a quiet, inoffensive necessity in that he performs the big majority of our rough work. . . . They have no effect on the American standard of living because they are not much more than a group of fairly intelligent Collie dogs."[3]

Dr. Roy L. Garis, a spokesperson for the eugenics movement, submitted a report to Representative John Box of Texas that quoted "an American living on the border" who described Mexicans as having "minds [that] run to nothing higher than animal functions—eat, sleep and sexual debauchery. . . . Yet there are Americans clamoring for more of this human swine." Mexican women were no longer viewed as "gay señoritas." Even "high-class Mexican women" were described in the same report as simply more "sneaky in adultery."[4]

There were no public hearings where Latinos could present their views. The Harris bill passed the Senate by voice vote. But by August 1930, so many Mexicans had left voluntarily to escape racism and unemployment that the bill was shelved. Close to three-quarters of the children who left were U.S.-born. Many didn't want to go, and some families were divided over the issue. Teenagers were especially upset. They resented separating from close friends and even sweethearts. But staying meant facing frequent harassment. Officials raided Mexican neighborhoods searching for "illegals." In Texas, vigilantes rousted people from their beds and shoved them over the border. The Brown Scare had returned with a vengeance.

Social agencies joined the game, albeit more subtly. When Mexican men and women lost their jobs, they were offered their transportation costs to the border. It was called "voluntary repatriation," but the families knew that if they refused to accept the offer there was a good chance that their relief checks would suddenly stop coming. To send a trainload of Mexicans to the border cost Los Angeles county a mere $77,000, compared with $348,000 to keep them on relief—a savings of $271,000 per trainload. About half a million men, women and children were deported, including thousands of Mexican U.S. citizens.[5]

By 1932, one out of four people in the United States could not find a job. When election day came in 1932, Herbert Hoover was resoundingly defeated by Franklin Delano Roosevelt, who had promised major efforts to end the depression. Roosevelt's so-called New Deal enacted laws that were frequently a disappointment to farm workers. The Agricultural Adjustment Act and the National Industrial Recovery Act excluded farm workers from important provisions such as the minimum wage, maximum hour standards, and prohibitions on child labor. When farmers were paid by the government to leave thousands of acres unplanted in order to keep prices high, farm workers were thrown off the land like so much excess baggage.

In recent years, Chicana scholars have interviewed women who participated in the struggles of the 1930s. These "oral histories" have given us precious firsthand recollections of the lives of working women who never achieved fame. Mrs. Rosaura Valdez (she used a pseudonym, preferring anonymity) told the scholars about her experiences during the 1933 cotton strike in California's San Joaquin Valley.

The strike began when producers of one-third of the nation's cotton banded together to set a starvation wage of forty cents per hundred pounds of picked cotton. When growers refused to negotiate with representatives of eighteen thousand workers, 80 percent of whom were Mexican, a strike date was set. The growers were ready. The Farmers Protective Association of Tulare promised them "armed aid" and called the strike "communist." Police and county sheriffs forcibly removed the strikers from their huts. The union had expected the evictions and had rented several camp sites. It was the best organized strike ever. The farm workers held elections and appointed committees to keep the camps clean, run schools for the children, set up strike kitchens, and even plan recreational events. The strikers strung barbed wire around each site and posted guards to prevent an "invasion."

Nine days after the strike began, hired goons fired on rallying and picketing farm workers. Three strikers were killed, among them a fifty-two-year-old mother and grandmother, Dolores Hernández. Eleven others were seriously wounded. Eight ranchers were tried and acquitted, but after a public outcry, Governor Rolph sent a fact-finding committee to the area. The officials admitted that the rights of the strikers had been violated and recommended small wage increases, but while the strikers considered the offer, their relief payments stopped coming.[6]

Rosaura Valdez went on to tell her interviewer how she and her husband, before the strike, spent their days in rows of cotton, their hands covered with cuts. No matter how hard they worked, they were always in debt to the company store. She picked about two hundred pounds of cotton in a ten-hour day. At the rate of pay the strikers were asking, she would have earned two dollars per day. She would fill a sack that was attached to her waist and hung between her legs. Next she picked up the hundred-pound sack, tossed it up on her shoulders and walked to a scale for weighing. There she would "put it back on my shoulder, climb a ladder up to a wagon and empty that sack in."[7]

About half the strikers at the largest camp were women. Rosaura Valdez herself was not a leader, but she remembered women speakers at rallies and many brave women who challenged strikebreakers. Lack of food was her clearest memory of the strike. Sometimes all they had was flour and water to prepare doughy pancakes and flat, tasteless breads. Children grew thin and pale, and at least one died of malnutrition. Growers hurled makeshift fire-bombs over the fence at night.

Thinking that men would not physically attack them, the women decided to take on the job of convincing the strikebreakers to leave the fields. Women with long hair and traditional Mexican peasant garments and younger women wearing modern American clothes rode together in trucks to the picket lines to heckle the strikebreakers. When talk failed, they armed themselves with pipes and knives, ripped up the cotton sacks of the "scabs," and emptied them onto the ground. Several of the women were beaten up, and most of the strikebreakers kept on working.

Mrs. Valdez's eyes sparkled when she talked about the women—"the real strikers," she called them. She emphasized that the women were braver than the men. She said she believed the strike was worth it. Wages went up each year after that.

When other growers cut wages, Mexican, Japanese, and impoverished white farm workers joined together in similar strikes. Sometimes they won a few concessions. More often they were forced to give in when their hungry children cried for food.[8]

The American Federation of Labor (AFL) had organized skilled workers into craft unions, but it had ignored the thousands who worked on production lines in auto, rubber, steel, and packinghouses. When the workers began organizing their own unions, the AFL sent in delegates of a committee for industrial organizations to lend a hand. Before long, they broke away from the AFL and founded the Congress of Industrial Organizations, the CIO.

The most serious problem facing all unions was the ready availability of thousands of unemployed people. Whenever the unions negotiated for better pay or working conditions, the employers had no problem finding hungry workers to replace them. In an Akron, Ohio, rubber tire plant in early 1936, during a drawn-out strike, the workers used a new tactic to prevent strikebreaking. Instead of leaving the plant and picketing outside, they sat down near their equipment and refused to leave. The employers were afraid to bring police into the plant for fear that machinery would be damaged. In a month the strike was won.

The new "sit-down" movement swept over the nation's industrial centers. In 1937, there were 477 sit-downs by auto workers, steel workers, and even gravediggers. In plants with women workers, the women were sent outside at night to picket, rather than subject the union to charges of holding wild parties inside the factories. Strikers were well aware of the kind of accusations anti-union newspapers could concoct. Committees were elected to organize meals and classes and provide sanitation facilities. College and high-school students came inside the plants to give courses in history and writing. Local shopkeepers and restaurant owners who depended on the workers for their livelihood donated meals and groceries.

As the union movement spread like wildfire, the Roosevelt administration acted to stabilize the situation by setting up the National Labor Relations Board. Unions were recognized as legitimate bargaining agents for the workers, and the NLRB helped prevent strikes through "collective bargaining" between employers and unions. Eventually, sit-down strikes were declared illegal, but the point had been made. Unions were around to stay.

The tactic of labeling strikers and their leaders "Reds," "Communists," and "un-American" did not work as well as it had during the days of the Palmer Raids. Working people were intent on bettering their lives, and if some of the organizers who came to help them were leftists—Communists, socialists, and anarchists—they didn't care. They heard stories from avowed Communists that the Soviet Union had not fallen victim to the worldwide depression. Others, who also called themselves Socialists or Trotskyists, agreed this was true but that Soviet premier Joseph Stalin also executed his opponents or sent them to slave labor camps. It was hard to sort it all out, but most of the workers paid little attention to such discussions as they fought to better their own lives. They knew that *anyone* who helped them was usually accused of being a "Red."

Latinos were active in most of the strikes and sitdowns of the 1930s. During steel strikes in Chicago in 1937, police killed ten workers and injured over a hundred when they fired on a pro-union parade on Memorial Day 1937. Mexican Americans from south Chicago's *barrios* comprised almost one-fifth of the marchers that day. Police referred to the parade as a "Mexican army."[9]

Lupe Marshall, a Chicana social worker, marched at the front of the parade. She took care of the wounded. Yet in accounts of those union-building days very few Chicanas are mentioned. As one scholar expressed it, "works on the Chicana are shrouded in myths. One of the most persistent of these is that she is a meek and subordinate creature who never ventures beyond the safety and confines of the home."[10] Another notes, "Contrary to the stereotype of the Hispanic Woman tied to the kitchen, most Mexican women, at some point in their lives, have been wage workers."[11]

In the 1930s in Chicago there were many households headed by widowed, divorced or separated Latinas. Most of them had worked in service occupations throughout the 1920s, but as the depression deepened, Latinas lost their jobs more often than any other group except African Americans. Many Chicanas and Mexican and Puerto Rican women attended English classes at free settlement houses or adult education programs, studying with immigrants from other countries. Latinas joined unemployed worker groups, unions, and neighborhood organizations where they mixed with women from Poland, Italy, and other countries and discovered that they had much in common—childrearing, poverty, "double duty" between jobs and home.

In Los Angeles, hundreds of Chicana and Mexican women were working in garment factories by the early 1930s, earning far less than the government-stipulated minimum wage. It took great courage for them to speak out. If they did, the owner could call the immigration authorities, and any woman without documents could be seized and deported. Despite these very real fears, they agreed to strike when an International Ladies Garment Workers Union (ILGWU) organizer, a Russian immigrant named Rose Pesotta, arrived and promised them union support.

The garment industry had grown since the 1890s, when throngs of eastern European Jewish immigrants came to New York and entered the apparel trades. The newcomers worked seven-day weeks and twelve-hour days for starvation wages. Many unions were organized but most didn't last long. The ILGWU was organized in 1900 by eleven male delegates. There were only a few women members and not much was accomplished until 1909 and 1910, when two Shirtwaist and Dressmakers' strikes took place. The second strike, called the "Great Revolt," involved about forty thousand workers and culminated in victory despite shocking police brutality against the picketers. In 1911, almost 150 young immigrant seamstresses, most of them Italian and Jewish, were burned to death in a tragic fire caused by unsafe conditions at the Triangle Shirtwaist Company. Union membership increased, and women organizers were hired to unionize in other cities as well as in Puerto Rico.

Local radio broadcasts reported fairly on the Los Angeles garment strike until advertisers pressured radio stations to stop. The Chicanas contacted a radio station across the border in Tijuana, and it beamed news of the garment workers' struggle to Spanish-speaking listeners all over southern California. Contributions flowed in and helped the women survive through two months of plant closures. By 1936, contracts had been signed with fifty-six dress manufacturers. Local 96 of the ILGWU, with a membership of more than three thousand mostly Mexican American women, joined the CIO.

Many Chicanas worked for years as union organizers, traveling all over the country. One of the best-known, Emma Tenayuca, got her start while she was still in high school in San Antonio, Texas. Born there in 1916, her maternal grandparents were one of the original Spanish families that founded the city. Her father was an Indian from South Texas. Emma joined the picket lines at Finck Cigar Company, where a hundred unionized workers were on strike. There she met and spent a night in jail with Mrs. W. H. Ernst, a Mexican who had founded the union. After graduating from high school, Tenayuca worked as an elevator operator and then helped Ernst form an organization for the unemployed, the Workers Alliance.

Wherever there was a strike, Tenayuca was there. In 1934 and 1935, she helped to organize two ILGWU locals in San Antonio. Becoming convinced of socialist ideas, she married a state organizer for the Communist party and joined the party herself. In early 1938 she became the spokesperson for two thousand pecan shellers who went out on strike under the banner of the United Cannery, Agricultural, Packing and Allied Workers of America (UCAPAWA). In a short time at least four thousand more women joined them on the picket lines. Two-thirds of the leaders of the strike were women. The workers were teargassed and arrested. The company finally gave in to most of the workers' demands, but the victory was short-lived. The industry quickly mechanized and fired all but one thousand workers. Concerned about Tenayuca's open support for the Communist party, the union replaced her with Luisa Moreno. The pecan shellers didn't agree with the decision. They elected Tenayuca as their honorary strike leader.[12]

In August 1939 Tenayuca organized a rally at the municipal auditorium. As the meeting was about to begin, over six thousand "ranchers, veterans, housewives, pig-tailed schoolgirls, skinny boys in high-heeled boots broke in yelling, 'Kill the dirty reds!'" Demoralized by the riot and too well-known as an organizer to land a job in San Antonio, Tenayuca left town. A Jewish woman who admired her labor activism found her a job sewing uniforms during World War II. Tenayuca later attended college in San Francisco and returned to San Antonio to teach school.

Manuela Solis Sager, who worked with Tenayuca during the 1938 pecan strike, had earlier organized garment and agricultural workers in Laredo, Texas. Working with her husband James Sager and other unionists, she organized a statewide conference in 1935 that established the South Texas Agricultural Workers Union. Manuela and her husband then organized field and packing shed workers in the Rio Grande Valley area.

Luisa Moreno, who replaced Tenayuca at UCA-PAWA, was from a very different background. Born in Guatemala, her middle-class parents were able to provide their children with many advantages. Moreno graduated from a Catholic college in California. But she was more interested in social causes than in a soft life.

Before Moreno became involved in the pecan workers' struggle in Texas, she worked as a seamstress in New York City and became an organizer for the AFL, organizing in the garment industry and then moving on to Florida to help Cuban cigar workers there. In 1937, she left her AFL job and went to work for the new and dynamic CIO, replacing Tenayuca.

Moreno faced her new job with optimism. By 1938, some 125,000 cannery and food processing workers had joined UCAPAWA, the seventh-largest union in the two-year-old CIO. The women who toiled in the canneries, most of them Chicanas, had everything to gain by becoming militant union members. Clustered together around tables and tubs, washing, grading, cutting, canning, and packing, the women were paid by the piece while the supervisors, always male, received hourly wages. Piecework was hated by all workers. It meant that in order to earn the barest living, everyone worked at an inhuman pace. Many women became the victims of sexual harassment by some of the supervisors.

At the California Sanitary Canning Company, known as Cal San, a peach canning plant, as elsewhere, grandmothers, daughters, and mothers lived under the same roof, traveled to work together, and pooled their money to pay the rent and keep food on the table. When more workers were needed, they brought other family members and friends to apply for the jobs. Experienced workers showed newcomers how to grade the peaches. They developed friendships and solidarity. In one plant the women joined together to start a child-care center right on the premises, predating the feminist demands of the 1970s by more than thirty years! Breaking with the tradition of unmarried young women living at home until the wedding bells rang, some of the women at the plant roomed together.

Mexican and Russian Jewish immigrant cannery workers lived in the same East Los Angeles neighborhoods, although on different blocks, meeting at bus stops at dawn. They developed a solidarity that made it possible for them to survive the hard times during their struggle to unionize. At Cal San, in 1937, the women had attempted unsuccessfully to organize an AFL local. Then Dorothy Ray Healey, a twenty-four-year-old CIO labor organizer, initiated a membership drive that signed up four hundred out of four hundred and thirty workers as members of UCAPAWA in less than three weeks. Despite the passage of the Wagner Act, legalizing the right of workers to unionize, the owners of Cal San refused to recognize the union or negotiate with the leaders. The women were demanding hiring of union members only (a closed shop), an end to the piece rate system, and the dismissal of most of the supervisors.

August is the height of the peach season, and on the last day of the month, in 1939, the women at Cal San walked out, leaving baskets of peaches to rot. Only fourteen stayed behind. Before the walkout the strikers had collected food from East Los Angeles grocers and asked them to refuse Cal San products as long as the strike continued. If the tradesmen refused, the women subjected them to chanting picket lines in front of their stores, known as a "secondary boycott." The International Brotherhood of Teamsters promised not to pick up and deliver Cal San goods. When some of the Teamsters broke their word, the women were not too shy to climb on the loading platform and pull down the pants of embarrassed truck drivers.

The NLRB sent arbitrators who blamed the employers for refusing to bargain with the union. But NLRB had no authority to force them to the conference table. For two and a half months, the women picketed and nothing happened. Then they tried an imaginative new tactic. Picketers appeared on the sidewalks in front of the owners' elegant homes. To the amazement of the upscale neighborhood, the marchers were skinny, ragged children, carrying signs with hand-printed messages like "I'm underfed because my Mama is underpaid." Some wealthy women, moved by the distressing sight, distributed food and beverages.

Under pressure from their own community, the owners finally met with union negotiators from the new UCAPAWA Local 75. The women won a closed shop, wage increases, and the firing of some of the most sexist foremen, but the hated piece rate system remained. In late 1940, Luisa Moreno worked with the Cal San unionists to organize other plants in the area and to initiate a campaign, rare in union history, to hire blacks. When World

70

War II created labor shortages, thirty black women were hired.[13]

Although the struggle for improved work conditions was the main focus of Latina activists, the issue of civil rights and educational equality remained important. LULAC concentrated on legal suits to end segregation in schools, restaurants, and hotels. It fought for the rights of Latinos to become members of juries and to remove hindrances to voting like poll taxes. At first concentrating on Texas, it began to respond to calls for aid in other parts of the nation.

Many of the telephone calls came from Latinas. Just as they were prominent in union organizing, women were often the first to seek a better education for their children. In 1934, still barring women from membership, LULAC introduced "Ladies Councils" for the official inclusion of women activists.

LULAC won occasional legal victories against owners of public accommodations who excluded Mexicans, but winning in court was one thing, enforcing the verdicts was another. As late as 1965, a dark-haired two-year-old girl, visiting her Chicano grandparents in Brownsville, Texas, approached a public swimming pool and cautiously put one foot into the water. Within seconds a pool attendant approached and told her harshly that she could not swim in the pool. Sitting nearby, her light-haired, blue-eyed mother walked over to see what was wrong. Her child was crying. The attendant became flustered. "You are her mother?" he asked. "I thought your daughter was Mexican." The mother allowed her daughter to swim in the pool but protested to the pool manager, who looked at his feet and mumbled.[14]

The first successful school segregation suit, long before the school desegregation decision of the Supreme Court in 1954, was won not by LULAC but by Latino parents in Lemon Grove, near San Diego, California.

Luisa Moreno also worked in these early Latino civil

rights struggles. She was not about to join a LULAC Ladies Council as a second-class citizen of the larger group. Furthermore, she believed that community action was more effective than legal suits. In 1938, along with Mexico-born Josefina Fierro de Bright, she founded the Spanish-Speaking Peoples Congress, known as El Congreso.[15]

Josefina Fierro de Bright was born in Mexico in 1920. Her parents came to California fleeing political persecution. Her mother, a PLM supporter, separated from her father when he returned to Mexico to fight in the armies of Pancho Villa. Josefina and her mother, Josefa Fierro, settled in Los Angeles, where Josefa opened a small restaurant that failed. Undaunted, Josefa bought a trailer and turned it into a sort of traveling restaurant and hotel for migrant farm workers. Josefina attended eight different schools during that period until her mother remarried and settled in a town in California's Central Valley.

Despite her fragmented early education, Josefina was an excellent student. In 1938, she attended the state university in Los Angeles. At a Latino nightclub where her aunt sang, she met and fell in love with John Bright, a radical novelist and Hollywood screenwriter. After their marriage, Josefina left school and began organizing in the Los Angeles Mexican community.

Factories and shops in the area would sell their products to Latinos, but they refused to hire them. Fierro de Bright organized consumer boycotts to force the hiring of Mexicans. With money from Latino Hollywood film stars like Anthony Quinn and Dolores Del Rio, she bought radio time to publicize the boycott.

Word of this dynamic young Latina reached Luisa Moreno, who contacted her to help establish El Congreso on December 4, 1938. At El Congreso's national convention, Josefina Fierro de Bright jubilantly addressed the crowd, telling them, "For the first time Mexican and Spanish American people have gathered together for unified action against the abuses of discrimination and poverty which have embittered and paralyzed them for so many years."[16] An excellent speaker in both Spanish and English, Fierro de Bright raised funds and went out on tours, speaking at meetings of Jewish clubs, African-American organizations, and the League of Women Voters. Under the leadership of Moreno and Fierro de Bright, El Congreso recruited about eighty thousand members, who mobilized against police abuse, deportations, and even the right of Spanish-speaking prisoners in San Quentin Penitentiary to exchange letters in Spanish with their families.

El Congreso organized a "hunger march" of twenty thousand people to the state capitol in Sacramento to protest the recently passed Swing Bill banning home relief to noncitizens "who made no effort to become citizens" (a status impossible to determine). The marchers gathered in front of the statehouse demanding that the governor veto the racist bill. Governor Olsen, looking down at the demonstrators outside, did just that.

Prior to its entry into World War II, the United States began expanding production of munitions, airplanes, trucks and tanks to assist the Soviet Union and Great Britain in their heroic defense against Hitler's war machine. One of El Congreso's last accomplishments before it became inactive in 1942, was the formation with Jewish and African-American organizations of the Council for the Protection of Minority Rights, demanding jobs for minorities in the newly opened, better-paying defense plants.

As millions of men went off to fight in Europe and the Pacific, women were hired for industrial jobs to replace the men. They were glorified (as shown in the film *Rosie the Riveter*) for their contribution to the war effort. Most of them were white.

Little was heard about some Latinas who, unable to get many jobs with the other "Rosie the Riveters," applied for jobs even more traditionally male than factory work.

73

They were hired as railroad workers by the Southern Pacific railroad and as miners in Arizona's copper mining camps.[17] Flossie Navarro told her story in 1989 to a journalist researching the mining strike of 1983 in those same mines.[18] She left her family farm in Arkansas in 1944 when she heard that the copper mines were hiring women. Mining work was far harder than the farm work she had done all her life. The workers on Flossie's shift were all women. Only the supervisors were male.

"Those women kept the mine going," she proudly said. As they walked through the streets of Clifton on their way to work, the women in their overalls and hard hats were labeled "prostitutes" by some of the townspeople. Quick-minded Flossie recalled how "I always said if I wanted to go and do such things I sure would find a nicer place to do them than in the muck and the water on that [mine smelter's] mill floor!"[19] A retired male miner, also remembering back, described how the mine owners at first brought in Jamaican men. After less than a year, he claimed, the Jamaicans left, saying the work was too hard. "But the women stayed." Another miner commented that the women were "among the best mine workers in the area. They were good, hard-to-earth women, and they didn't take no bull."[20]

No mining union was interested in bringing the women in as members, so they organized strikes on their own. During one of these "wildcat strikes" (strikes not endorsed by an official union) they protested sexual harassment by foremen after two women were discharged for "flirting." Firings were common when women resisted advances by their supervisors.

After the war, the owners tried to fire the women, claiming that they weren't strong enough to do the heavy work! For a short time, the mining women held on to their jobs, as did the "Rosies" in the defense plants, but in the end they gave the jobs back to the men. It wasn't until 1973 that a new generation of women were hired at the mines after a victorious union-backed equal opportunity lawsuit. Some of the newly hired women thought they were the first ones. Only a few knew about the Latina copper miners of World War II.

In the war years, not many well-paying jobs were given to Latinas or Latinos. The Latinas in the food processing plants gave ample evidence of their abilities as wartime workers. As part of the "Food for Victory program," they produced at unprecedented levels and donated money and blood for the war effort. They also convinced some of the companies to finance day-care centers on the premises.[21]

In the fields where the crops destined for the canneries were grown, a shortage of labor developed as Mexican Americans went off to war and Japanese agricultural workers were herded off to detention camps along with the rest of the nation's Japanese. The growers wanted to open the border doors wide so that an excess of migrants from Mexico could compete with one another to keep wages down. The Mexican government insisted on a contract that at least spelled out some basic wage rates and guarantees against discrimination for the so-called *braceros* (working hands). Congress passed the Bracero Program honoring Mexico's wishes, declaring braceros to be "vital to the war effort."

Hundreds of thousands of Mexicans were contracted, most for farm work and almost sixty-eight thousand to keep the railroads running. The stipulations of the agreement with Mexico were violated more frequently than they were obeyed. Braceros lived under inhuman conditions, worked long hours, and suffered endless racist acts of humiliation. Luisa Moreno and her Council for the Protection of Minority Rights protested, but to little avail. The Mexican government refused for a long time to send contract workers to Texas, so flagrant was the racism.[22]

In most public places in California and the Southwest, not only braceros but also Mexican American mili-

75

tary personnel faced NO MEXICANS signs in many establishments. Despite the fact that almost half a million Mexican Americans fought bravely during World War II, winning more congressional medals of honor than any other ethnic group, racism did not diminish. The Nazis emphasized that they were the "Aryan race," superior to all others. Their massive extermination campaign against Jews, the largest minority in Europe, was making headlines. Many Americans became more conscious of the terrible consequences of racism but still victimized Latinos and African Americans. One of the most publicized incidents of anti-Latino racism culminated with a full-scale race riot in Los Angeles in 1943—the so-called zoot-suit riots.

For most of the century, young men and teenagers had formed ethnically based clubs in the cities—Polish American, Italian American, and so on. They wore outfits to distinguish themselves from other groups and warred against one another occasionally, usually over girls. Latinos, under the pressure of discrimination and poverty, also sought comfort, unity, and sometimes even a substitute for broken families in their neighborhood clubs.[23] In California, Latino club members were called "zoot-suiters" for their flaring pants and long jackets. Los Angeles newspapers ran frequent incendiary articles on the alleged "threat" of these boisterous but usually harmless groups.

In the summer of 1942, a fight between two gangs led to the death of one young man and the indictment of twenty-four Mexican American youngsters picked up at random by the police. The boys' parents contacted Josefina Fierro de Bright, and she raised money for legal help and organized the Sleepy Lagoon Defense Committee. Despite evidence to the contrary, nine young men were convicted of second-degree murder charges and sent off to jail. Convinced of their innocence, Fierro de Bright continued raising money for an appeal. In 1944 the district court of appeals reversed the conviction of all the defendants, but the anti-Mexican barrage in the press did not stop.

In June 1943, while the Sleepy Lagoon defendants were still locked in jail, sailors and marines on leave, perhaps after first quenching their thirst in local bars, filled the streets of downtown Los Angeles, beating up "zoot-suiters" and anyone with dark skin, calling them "greasers and niggers," and treating Latinas like prostitutes. On June 7, the riot escalated as the mob entered bars, movie theaters, and restaurants in search of Mexicans, African Americans and Filipinos.

Fierro de Bright commented later that the riot was the "most horrifying experience of my time. I dreamed about it for months afterwards." She flew immediately to Washington and appealed to the Roosevelt adminstration to take steps to end the racism by military personnel. In her bag were clippings documenting the incendiary press articles that she believed had incited the rioters. A short while later, the Navy Department ordered its men to remain out of the Mexican neighborhoods. It was the last of Fierro de Bright's victories. She was soon forced to leave the country.[24]

All during the Second World War, the U.S. government and Hollywood produced films applauding the courage of the Russian people. Films like *The North Star,* produced in 1943, featuring box office favorites Anne Baxter and Dana Andrews and still listed in film books today as a "four star" movie, pictured brave Russians fighting off the Nazi invaders and a typical Russian family that looked and behaved exactly like white American families, including even squabbling and flirting teenage children.[25]

Within a year after the war, the alliance between the two great powers deteriorated into a cold war that was to continue until the Soviet Union's collapse in 1990. Already in 1946 American leaders were portraying the former Soviet ally as a threat to the security of the United

States. It was claimed that American Communists had secretly infiltrated the government and other institutions in a plot to destroy the United States from within. Julius and Ethel Rosenberg, a husband and wife, were executed in the electric chair for allegedly passing atomic bomb secrets to the Soviets, a charge that is disputed to this day. An irrational fear of the "Communist menace" swept the country.

During World War II industrialists had grown very rich from war profits while unions took "no strike" pledges so as not to curtail production; members had received few increases in their wages. Right after the war, massive strikes swept the nation's industrial centers as war heroes returned and demanded not only ticker tape parades but their share of the gravy. Some historians conclude that the industrialists decided that the best way to break the power of the unions was to dust off the old Red-baiting tactic and create a new enemy, Communist Russia. In this way the nation could also continue producing armaments and avoid falling back into an economic depression.

Critics of the cold war foreign policy of President Harry Truman point out that the Soviet Union was scarcely a threat. Nazi armies had invaded and destroyed much of its industrial capacity. Millions of Russian citizens had been slaughtered. The war-weary Russians were calling for peaceful coexistence, a chance to rebuild their war-torn nation.

The voices of peace and moderation were quickly drowned out by a national anticommunist hysteria called the "witch-hunt" and "McCarthyism," after Senator Joseph McCarthy. The senator gained notoriety for his hearings demanding that hundreds of people testify about their "Communist" activities and name people who they believed were also "Reds." A list of "subversive" organizations compiled by Attorney General A. Mitchell Palmer during the Palmer Raids in 1919 was dusted off and revised. By 1948 it listed seventy-eight organizations, including any groups that had fought for the defense of prisoners, trade unions, civil rights, and immigrant rights. President Harry Truman vetoed the McCarran Internal Security Act of 1950, that would have permitted massive deportations and jailings of dissenters and authorized the construction of "emergency" concentration camps, but Congress overruled his veto. The act was originally drafted with the help of Richard Nixon of California. Another law, the McCarran-Walter Immigration and Nationality Act of 1952, allowed for the "denaturalizing" of naturalized citizens on political grounds. They could be arrested without a warrant, held without bail, and deported for belonging to one of the listed organizations.[26]

Latinos in the barrios became frequent victims of the witch-hunt as lawmen swooped down on entire families and shipped them over the border. Anyone who defended the deportees was accused of being "un-American," dupes of the "Reds," or "Reds" themselves. Labor's best leaders were thrown out of their unions, leaving behind those who would rarely defend workers' rights. Individuals who had signed a petition or even attended a meeting of one of the blacklisted organizations could lose their jobs without ever facing their accusers.

LULAC did not protest the witch-hunt and was the only civil rights organization seemingly untouched by McCarthyism. The organization had frequently affirmed its patriotic and anticommunist stance. It had nothing to say when El Congreso leader Luisa Moreno was deported, or when Fierro de Bright left the United States rather than provide the names of supposed "Communists" or friends of Communists to the House Un-American Activities Committee. Her husband left with her, also persecuted during McCarthy's televised hearings of the film industry.[27]

By the time Moreno was deported, she was international vice president of the United Cannery, Agricultural, Packing and Allied Workers of America and state vice president of the CIO. Giving in to the witch-hunt, the CIO expelled the UCAPAWA union in 1950 on the grounds of "Communist domination." With Moreno and several other leaders deported or fired, cannery workers were ordered to join the Teamsters. If they refused, they were fired and their names were put on a list circulated to all canneries and food processing plants so that no one would hire them again. The women of the canneries would never again have the favorable conditions they had fought so hard for and won in the 1930s, including a health care plan. Years later, one of the Cal San workers insisted, "UCAPAWA was the greatest thing that ever happened to the workers at Cal San. It changed everything and everybody."[28]

Among the handful of those who fought back against the witch-hunt's repressive policies, Mexican Americans were prominent. Three Latino civil rights groups actually *began* during that time of severe thought control: the American GI Forum, the Community Service Organization (CSO), and the Asociación Nacional México-Americana (ANMA—National Mexico-American Association).[29]

Future farm-worker organizer Dolores Huerta, as well as Cesar Chavez, were active in the CSO (*see* chapter 5). The CSO helped organize California's Civic Unity Leagues that ran Mexican American political candidates—a rare event. The leagues welcomed women, who played leading roles in voter registration drives.

Women were an even more important part of ANMA. The predominantly Latino International Union of Mine, Mill and Smelter Workers (known as Mine-Mill), founded in the Arizona mining triangle early in the century, became part of the CIO in the 1930s. Even as the CIO threw out UCAPAWA, it expelled Mine-Mill. But despite the expulsion, the miners remained loyal to their union, refusing to toss out their leadership. ANMA was founded in 1949 by union members and their families and friends to protect the civil rights of miners and other workers. Unlike LULAC, ANMA welcomed noncitizens as well as citizens. Local chapters sprang up in various parts of the country. Many women were elected to office. Isabel González, a leader of migrant workers and the unemployed, was elected as the first vice president. After her untimely death a few months later, Celia Rodriguez was elected, along with other women officers.

Julia Luna Mount, one of the women elected, was a cannery worker and organizer for UCAPAWA who joined El Congreso and worked in an airplane factory during the war. She had also been active in support of the young Mexican American men thrown in jail during the Sleepy Lagoon case. She openly opposed the witch-hunt before joining ANMA. Made up of thousands of courageous members like Luna Mount, ANMA was the only major civil rights organization in the nation to publicly speak out against the cold war and the many violations of the precious civil liberties guaranteed by the Bill of Rights.[30]

After the Korean War of 1950-1953 pulled the country out of a brief recession, the economy went into another slump. Mexican workers were again scapegoated for the downturn. During "Operation Wetback," a million and a half Mexicans were deported, including many citizens.[31] ANMA once more spoke out—a solitary voice in a hurricane of injustice. ANMA finally collapsed in 1954 after years of being hounded by the FBI, but its courage during the dark days of McCarthyism is now well recognized.

In the early 1950s, Mine-Mill went on a fifteen-month strike in New Mexico against Empire Zinc. Because the men had backed up any woman who wished to keep her wartime job in the mine, the women remained loyal to the union. When injunctions under the new anti-union Taft-Hartley law prevented miners from picketing, the women blocked strikebreakers from the mine. They were thrown in jail, but the union won a partial victory.

This strategy would be repeated more than thirty years later during a mining strike against Phelps Dodge Copper in 1983 (*see* chapter 6). Latina women's militant role in the Empire Zinc strike was portrayed in the film *Salt of the Earth* made by independent (and witch-hunted) filmmakers in 1954. Latino actors as well as miners played the roles of the strikers in the film. Film distributors refused to show the movie that went on to win critical acclaim when the witch-hunt ended.

Organizers like Luisa Moreno had often talked about other Latinas living in the United States—Spanish-speaking women from Puerto Rico, most of them living in New York City, some in Chicago. Mexican American war veterans also mentioned Puerto Rican soldiers who had fought beside them during the fierce battles in the South Pacific and Europe. During World War II many more Puerto Ricans had come to the United States. Thousands of miles separated the majority of Chicanas and "Puertorriqueñas," but more and more over the next exciting decade of the 1960s they would meet and find out how much they had in common besides the Spanish language.

4

cuatro

To the
Land of
Ice and
Snow

In the Southwest, Mexicans and Mexican Americans enjoyed a mild climate that reminded them of home—*México lindo* (beautiful Mexico). Only a few brave souls reluctantly traipsed off to live battered by the freezing winds of Chicago. Cubans headed for sunny Florida when they fled political persecution in the nineteenth century, returning home as soon as there was hope for a better life.

The story of the second-largest group of Latinos in the United States, the Puerto Ricans, is very different. The island of Puerto Rico, like its neighbors in the Caribbean, is a lush tropical island, about 100 miles long and 35 miles wide. It has beautiful beaches fronting the warm waters of the Caribbean Sea. The interior boasts an amazing variety of rain forests, mountains, and rich soil.

When the Spanish conqueror Juan Ponce de León arrived early in the sixteenth century, he found peaceful agricultural Indians who called their home Boriquen, "land of the great lord." He and his soldiers enslaved the Indians. Within a generation, almost all the Indians died from overwork, defeated rebellions, or diseases brought by Europeans. Hoping to find gold, the Spaniards named the island "rich port" (Puerto Rico). But the largest gold and silver deposits were in Mexico and Peru, and so Puerto Rico remained a backwater of the Spanish Empire, used mostly as a resting place for merchant and slave ships in transit.

The French colony of Haiti had been a major producer of sugar. After Caribbean sugar cultivation dwindled because of Haiti's revolution against France during the early years of the nineteenth century, Spanish rulers decided to take up the slack by growing more sugar in Puerto Rico and Cuba. In Cuba, sugar rapidly became a full-fledged industry, displacing farmers, turning them into laborers. Hundreds of thousands of African slaves were used to cut the sugarcane. In Puerto Rico, sugar was grown on family type haciendas. Along with thirty thousand slaves, about a million subsistence farmers worked at the haciendas but earned very little cash. On *la pieza de los pobres* (the piece of land of the poor), the men and women grew food for their families, raised chickens, pigs, and goats, and made their own molasses and rum.[1] Although most Latin American colonies had won independence in the early 1820s, Spain tenaciously held on to Cuba and Puerto Rico. Slaves launched hundreds of guerrilla attacks against their Spanish tormenters. Southern growers and northern businessmen in the United States, eager to acquire Spain's colonies, began investing there. They made fortunes building railways, communication systems, and steam-operated sugar refineries, using the labor of slaves and low-paid Cubans and Puerto Ricans.

By 1865, Cuban and Puerto Rican exiles in New York City and in Key West and Tampa, Florida, were working together in the antislavery Republican Society of

Cuba and Puerto Rico, raising funds to arm the independence movements in their homelands. On September 23, 1868, a group of freedom fighters took up arms in the mountain town of Lares, and descended to San Sabastían, where they proclaimed the "First Republic of Puerto Rico" and demanded the abolition of slavery. Puerto Ricans to this day celebrate that date in September as *El Grito de Lares* (the Cry of Lares). But the rebels' action was quickly suppressed, and their leader, Betances, fled to the safety of the exile community in New York City. Some scholars assert that the revolt attracted so much support that the Spanish rulers were compelled to emancipate the slaves five years later. Others point out that slavery had outlived its usefulness because the sugar industry had declined sharply in Puerto Rico.

With Spain having serious problems keeping control in the Caribbean, Secretary of State James Blaine wrote to President Benjamin Harrison in 1891 that he saw "only three places that are of value to be taken: one is Hawaii and the others are Cuba and Puerto Rico."[2] But first they would have to deal with Spain.

José Martí, known as the great Cuban Liberator, headed the Cuban Revolutionary party. The party received immense support from Cuban tobacco workers in Tampa, Florida, many of them women. By 1897, Cuba's guerrillas were gaining the upper hand. Unable to fight a war on the two separate islands of Cuba and Puerto Rico, Spain granted Puerto Rico autonomy. The Cubans, tasting victory, refused to make a deal with Spain.

Puerto Rico was granted the Autonomous Charter of 1897 in order to prevent it from joining the Cubans and to keep the Autonomista Party and its followers loyal to Spain.

In February 1898, in the dead of night in the harbor of Havana, Cuba, a mysterious explosion destroyed the U.S. battleship *Maine*. Some historians believe that U.S. agents destroyed the ship to justify a war with Spain. On

April 25, 1898, the United States declared war on Spain, even though Spain, defeated by the guerrillas, made a last-minute offer to cede Cuba to the United States. The United States refused to accept Spain's offer of Cuba and face angry ex-slaves who had just liberated themselves. The United States intended to win an easy war against Spain and, by extension, the guerillas.[3] In ten weeks Spain turned over Cuba and the Philippines to a victorious United States. The guerrillas knew they had no chance of defeating their new "liberators."

When the Spanish authorities hesitated to include autonomous Puerto Rico in the deal, U.S. troops quickly invaded the island. The Treaty of Paris signed in December 1898 granted independence to Cuba but gave Puerto Rico, the Philippines, and Guam to the United States. No Puerto Rican was present to object to the "gift-giving." The Spanish flag was replaced with the Stars and Stripes, waving under the breezes of "Manifest Destiny!"

Some Puerto Ricans had assumed that democratic self-government would be theirs as soon as the United States liberated the area from Spain. A U.S. government press release told the real story: "Puerto Rico will be kept. . . . Once taken, it will never be released."[4] For two years military commanders ruled the country. In 1900, the Foraker Act provided for a U.S.-appointed governor. The Puerto Rican people were not permitted to elect their own governor until 1948! In the schools, teachers taught lessons in English, and children pledged allegiance to the American flag. A resident commissioner represented the island in the U.S. House of Representatives but was not permitted to vote in Congress. A bicameral legislature that existed on the island had little power.

Within a few decades, as investors poured money into the island, family-centered sugar haciendas gave way to modern, highly profitable sugar plantations. This had an enormous impact on the Puerto Rican people. Like their Mexican counterparts in the Southwest, they lost access to the land, the source of their survival crops, and were forced to work for wages on the plantations. Substandard wages could not buy the overpriced food products imported from the United States. After 1900, ownership of sugar plantations was in the hands of five huge American companies.

To make matters even worse, the sugar mills and fields were mechanized, which reduced the number of jobs available. Five thousand Puerto Rican farm workers were transferred to Hawaii in 1900. As the decades passed, more and more Puerto Rican agricultural workers went to U.S. farms along the East Coast during harvest season and to work as cotton pickers in Arizona.[5]

In the early 1900s, a union movement emerged, calling itself the Free Federation of Workers—FLT. Active in its leadership was a woman, Luisa Capetillo. Born in 1879 in Arecibo, Puerto Rico, she was a teenager when her beloved country was "given" to the United States by Spain. Self-educated, she became particularly concerned about the problems of working women and wrote dramas and articles protesting women's subordination. She was the first woman on the island to wear slacks in public—an act of defiance—while she walked the picket lines of the tobacco workers in 1907. In 1910, she joined the staff of the FLT newspaper and traveled to New York and Florida to consult with exiles. During an agricultural strike in 1918, she was arrested. All the while she raised three children. Her hard life took its toll. She died of tuberculosis in 1922 at the age of 43.[6]

Until recently, almost nothing was written about the first Puerto Rican settlements in the United States. According to a leading Puerto Rican scholar, "social scientists . . . blatantly denied the existence of an early Puerto Rican community and failed to perceive the relationship between early support systems or coping institutions and the later migration."[7]

It worked like a column of building blocks, each

block supporting the next. Just as early Mexican settlers had done, when newcomers arrived the original settlers helped them find housing and jobs and provided a "family" feeling. Merchants were the first Puerto Ricans to come to the United States in the early 1800s. Spain's colonies had been allowed to trade only with the "mother country." Puerto Rican and Cuban merchants engaged in illegal trade with the United States, smuggling in sugar and molasses to New York and New England in exchange for basic food-stuffs and manufactured goods needed at home.

By 1830, Puerto Rican merchants in New York City had formed a Spanish Benevolent Society that helped newcomers adjust and fed them when their businesses failed. They were joined by a few students and political exiles who, like the PLM Mexican revolutionaries, published newspapers that were banned in Cuba and Puerto Rico. In 1895 they formed a branch of the Cuban Revolutionary party. Working alongside them was a racially integrated group of women, La Liga Antillana. Because of their mixed-race membership, they had difficulty renting meeting halls in New York City.[8]

There were up to twenty thousand Puerto Ricans living in forty-four states by 1920, most of them in a few New York City neighborhoods. The thousands of new arrivals, like those from Cuba, the Dominican Republic, and Spain, depended on the *colonia hispana* (the name they gave Spanish-speaking neighborhoods) to house them, help them overcome language barriers, and find jobs. Most of the newcomers were workers, sometimes recruited in Puerto Rico by American companies looking for cheap labor. As immigrants in all parts of the nation were doing, these immigrants formed mutual aid societies and social clubs that raised funds for hungry families.[9]

There was a small group of professionals in the barrio, not comprising more than 3 percent of the Latino population at any given time. The 1923 *Guia Hispana*

(Spanish Guide) listed 150 professionals, most of them male. But two women were identified as Spanish instructors at Columbia University[10] during this period when very few women of any race or ethnic group were able to enter the worlds of professions and businesses except as clerks and elementary school teachers.

As they are doing today, most of the Latina professionals made an important contribution to their communities. In the early 1920s, Pura Belpré, an expert in folklore, was the first Puerto Rican librarian in the New York City public library system. She established special programs emphasizing Puerto Rican culture at the Harlem branch of the public library and arranged storytelling hours in Spanish for neighborhood children.

Sister Carmelita Bonilla, a Trinitarian nun from Puerto Rico, encouraged many young Hispanics in the Brooklyn barrio to concentrate on their studies. She was one of the founders of Casita Maria, a settlement house, and often acted as an intermediary between the Latino settlers and non-Hispanics.[11]

Few left the warm lands of their birth out of choice. As underpaid as they were in the wintry north, it was more than they could earn in Puerto Rico. Skilled seamstresses, cigar makers, and factory workers formed settlements in the Lower East Side and Chelsea neighborhoods of New York City, near their workplaces. Their neighbors were eastern European and Italian immigrants.

One of the earliest neighborhoods developed in the waterfront area of Brooklyn, near the Navy Yard, when the American Manufacturing Company contracted 130 young women from Puerto Rico. To convince their parents to let them leave, the company set them up in a group of three-story modernized buildings, where "chaperons from well-known respected Puerto Rican families" watched over them. A free bus took them to work and back. Others came to the area, and small family-run businesses catering to Latino tastes sprang up—*bodegas* (grocery stores), restaurants, beauty shops, and the first take-out restaurant in the city.

The largest early *colonia* developed in what soon was called "El Barrio" or "Spanish Harlem" in Manhattan's East 90s on the fringe of African American Harlem. In 1916, the Puerto Rican residents of El Barrio were in the minority among poor Jewish and Italian families.

In all of the Latino neighborhoods, homesick people exchanged news about Puerto Rico. Puerto Rican leaders on the island and in New York pressured Congress to end colonial control of Puerto Rico, but Congress continued to ignore the situation. When, however, the United States needed men to fight in Europe during World War I, Congress passed the Jones Act, making Puerto Ricans U.S. citizens and therefore eligible for the draft. Within a month eighteen thousand young Puerto Ricans joined the U.S. armed forces.

Not many people were fooled by their new "citizenship" status. They could not vote in U.S. presidential elections. Those in the United States theoretically could vote in local elections, but difficult and culturally biased literacy tests in English made it impossible for most. Puerto Rico's legislature and its supreme court justices appointed by the United States had little power. "The government of Puerto Rico, in effect, governs practically nothing," a leading scholar has observed.[12]

Nevertheless, Puerto Ricans continued to stream into New York to find jobs. The trip by steamship cost between twenty-five and fifty-five dollars, depending on the accommodations, and took three to five days. For young women like Rosa Roma, it was something of an adventure in 1926.

> . . . *I paid fifty-five dollars for the voyage to New*
> *York and the ship was the* Coamo. *We were*
> *seasick. I don't remember much about food service.*

But I do remember I was traveling second-class and
there were some students traveling on first—
Spaniards. We flirted with them, talked with
them—they brought us pastries and fruits from first
class.[13]

That year the *New York Times* reported there were between 150,000 and 200,000 Puerto Ricans in the United
States, the majority crammed into *El Barrio.* Pushcarts
clogged Park Avenue, offering bargain clothing and
leather goods in an open-air market. Soon vendors added
Latino foods to their wares—*platanos* (a banana-like fruit)
and many varieties of beans. On 110th Street, stores with
fancier merchandise drew window-shoppers and better-
paid workers. Most Puerto Ricans from Brooklyn hopped
the bus to El Barrio to shop or visit doctors on days off.
Downtown, on West 14th Street, the restaurant of El Hotel Latino served Spanish cuisine.

It was still not home. Puerto Rican leaders continued to press the independence cause and were told in no
uncertain terms that they were an inferior people inca-
pable of self-government. A 1928 resolution by the
Puerto Rican legislature sent a message to President Calvin Coolidge that cited "the cry of Patrick Henry—'Lib-
erty or Death!' " and called on him to "grant us the freedom that you enjoy . . . which we deserve and you have
promised us."[14] President Coolidge responded with an
angry letter rejecting the suggestion that Puerto Rico
could survive on its own:

We found the people of Porto Rico [sic—U.S.
authorities changed the name of Puerto Rico to Porto
Rico in 1900 because they could not pronounce the
correct name] . . . ignorant, poverty-stricken and
diseased, not knowing what constituted a free and
democratic government and without the experience of
having participated in any government. . . . [It is]

*unreasonable to suggest that the people of Porto
Rico . . . will progress . . . isolated from the source
from which they have received practically their only
hope of progress.*[15]

Faced with this kind of racism whenever they ventured
outside of their barrios, the new "citizens" were well aware
that they were not welcomed in the United States. Nevertheless, the economic conditions in Puerto Rico had
made coming to the icy streets of the North a necessity
for many. Even though American industrialists had
opened factories throughout the island, wages were so low
and prices of imported foods so high that hunger was a
common visitor in many homes. In 1929, Luis Muñoz
Marín, who would later be elected the first Puerto Rican
governor of the island, wrote an article in an American
magazine commenting bitterly:

*The American flag found Porto Rico penniless and
content. It now flies over a prosperous factory worked
by slaves who have lost their land and may soon lose
their guitars and their songs. In the old days most
Porto Rican peasants owned a few pigs and chickens,
maybe a horse or a cow, some goats, and in some
way had the use of a patch of soil. . . . While there
are many more schools for their hungry children and
many more roads for their bare feet, their destiny is
decidedly narrower now. . . .*[16]

After Congress enacted legislation setting strict quotas on
immigrants from anywhere other than northwestern Europe, jobs became more available for Puerto Ricans traveling to the United States. But they were usually the most
unpleasant jobs. While white men and women waited
tables in restaurants, Puerto Ricans washed dishes and
cleared tables. While white women waited on customers
in dress shops, Puerto Rican women unpacked heavy
crates in back rooms. Even more worked in dismal fac-

tory buildings, always worrying that the ancient structures would go up in flames. Still, a rotten job was better than no job at all at home.

While women everywhere were being told that their place was in the home, twenty-five percent of the Puerto Rican women in the United States during the decade of the twenties worked at a wide variety of outside jobs. There were cigar makers and *lectores* (readers of newspapers, short stories and poetry to the workers in cigar factories), maids and baby-sitters, typists, lacemakers, seamstresses, and washerwomen in steamy laundries.

Spanish-language want ads appeared asking for pieceworkers, women who would sew at home. In Puerto Rico, many of the women had worked as skilled embroiderers and lacemakers while their children played out in the sunshine. Now, surrounded by children stuck indoors in confined quarters with cold, dangerous streets outside, mothers took home bundles of materials and worked late into the night making a few dollars to add to the family survival income. They created artificial flowers, lamp shades, and even jewelry. In a good week, they could earn about ten dollars. A few enterprising women bought the materials themselves and sold their work door to door. All over El Barrio, lace doilies covered scratches on battered dressers, and homemade lamp shades cut the glare from dime-store lamps.

Many women provided home day care for the children of working relatives and neighbors. Often they raised the children of sick or deceased relatives or friends. In El Barrio, there were seldom homeless babies. The tradition of *compadrazgo* (godparents) came to mean communal responsibility for young people. This caring behavior often extended to adult relatives as well. Almost every family in the barrio had near or distant relatives living with them most of the time. When newcomers were due to arrive, the news traveled through an informal women's information network. Over sewing machines in factories, on front stoops in summer, and in church or in schoolyards when they went to pick up their children, women discussed jobs that the new members of the barrio might land and apartments with room for a boarder or two.

One woman who lived in the barrio during that time remembered when she was ten and a cousin moved out, leaving her a tiny but beautifully decorated room of her own. Some weeks later the doorbell rang and when she opened the door she saw:

> . . . the couple standing there and the baby held in its mother's arm. They were an uncle I had never met, his wife . . . and their infant son. They had arrived without warning from Puerto Rico on the asumption that if there is room for one there is always room for one more. My heart sank as I remembered my father's favorite value—you never turn away relatives, no matter how little you have for yourself. I knew instinctively they would be well received and my room with the matching blue spread and curtains would be given to them for as long as they needed it.[17]

Along with this cooperative network, a few dozen organizations existed in the Brooklyn and Manhattan *colonias*. The Puerto Rican Brotherhood, founded in 1923, was the largest, defending Puerto Ricans against racism and keeping a close watch on events in Puerto Rico. After a riot over "turf" on the streets of Harlem between African American and Latino youth during the hot days of July 1926, the brotherhood played an important role in calming things down. Women were very active in La Liga Puertorriqueña e Hispana. They represented the community in discussions with the city administration, demanding improvements in the barrio schools and the abolition of the literacy test for voters.

Although researchers who underplay the importance of these early Puerto Rican barrios also claim that Puerto

Ricans had no interest in elections, an estimated seven thousand registered Puerto Rican voters participated in the 1918 election of Governor Alfred E. Smith. In 1927, the congressman from East Harlem and future mayor of New York City, Fiorello La Guardia, asked Puerto Rican leaders for advice about possible legislation of interest to Puerto Ricans. Bilingual Puerto Rican women functioned as poll watchers and interpreters. In the next decades they would become even more politically active in the campaigns of Franklin D. Roosevelt for the presidency and their own congressman, Vito Marcantonio. Puerto Ricans were interested in politicians who were willing to go to bat for them, not in the machinations of party bosses who ruled New York City.[18]

This became especially important during the hard times of the 1930s Great Depression, when Latinos and African Americans suffered even more unemployment, evictions, and outright hunger than most other Americans. Thousands of Puerto Ricans were forced to apply for home relief. Activists in Unemployed Councils fought to make sure that hungry people were not turned away by bureaucrats working at the Department of Welfare. After Roosevelt was elected in 1932, government programs like the Works Progress Administration provided a few jobs for Latinos. They were paid just the minimum needed to stay alive. But most of the jobs went to unemployed white workers, swelling the relief rolls in African American and Latino neighborhoods. As the middle-class population of the city cut back on their own spending on nonessentials, even fewer jobs were available for thousands of Latino restaurant and hotel workers, garment workers, and those employed as servants in upper-class homes. When Roosevelt's New Deal administration included Puerto Rico in its programs, setting up the Puerto Rico Reconstruction Administration, many barrio families left for home where they could also get home relief but at least didn't need winter clothes for their children. In Puerto

Rico they found even more deplorable conditions, causing people to move back and forth between the island and the mainland in desperate quest for work.

Despite the hard times, the people of the barrio found ways to enjoy life. Local movie houses featured films from Argentina and Mexico, and in vaudeville houses Spanish-speaking comedians made audiences laugh and briefly forget their troubles. Young Latinos attended dances in halls like the Audubon Ballroom in the African American section of Harlem where the owners sometimes hired Latino bands to bring in customers from El Barrio. In their homes, on battered phonographs, families listened to Latino singers and musicians on Columbia and RCA Victor records bought at local family-run record stores. When a family was unable to pay the rent, women would spread the word and neighbors would hold rent parties, charging a small admission and turning the proceeds over to the frightened tenants.

Some turned to religion for comfort, but the Catholic church in the North duplicated its policy in the Southwest by failing to bring many Latinos into the priesthood. In church, the white, English-speaking priests instructed their parishioners to Americanize and keep away from "troublemakers," a code word for those who engaged in social protest. Many barrio women raised their children as nominal Catholics, sticking to the minimal requirements of the Church. Others brought their old religion, and African-based forms of spiritism and spiritualism merged with elements of Catholicism and became known as Santería. Some were attracted to Protestant evangelistic sects like the Pentacostalists, who preached in Spanish, and used music during emotional Sunday services.[19]

Latina poetess Judith Ortiz Cofer has written about the experiences of Latinas attending churches where the priests spoke in English:

Latin women pray
in incense sweet churches;
they pray in Spanish to an Anglo God
with a Jewish heritage.

And this Great White Father,
imperturbable on His marble pedestal,
looks down upon His brown daughters
votive candles shining like lust
in His all seeing eyes,
unmoved by their persistent prayers.

Yet year after year
before His image they kneel,
Margarita, Josefina María and Isabel,
all fervently hoping
that if not omnipotent,
at least He be bilingual. [20]

Whatever the advice of priests and ministers, the women of the barrios refused to remain silent when urgent issues arose in Puerto Rico or in New York. They organized and searched for supporters, regardless of their nationality. One man they came to regard as a true friend was Italian American Vito Marcantonio. Raised in the Italian area of East Harlem, Marcantonio became congressman for Harlem's Twentieth Assembly District, which incorporated El Barrio. Latinos dubbed him "Puerto Rico's congressman" and helped reelect him to Congress from 1938 to 1950.

Marcantonio won the affection of hundreds of Latina mothers in 1935 when they felt that their children were under attack. The Special Committee on Immigration and Naturalization of the Chamber of Commerce of the State of New York administered intelligence tests in English designed for middle-class white children to 156 Puerto Rican school children. Afterwards, they announced that Puerto Rican children had "significantly lower IQs than

American-born white children" and that they were "mentally deficient" and "intellectually immature."

Josefina Silva de Cintrón, who founded in 1933 the literary journal *Revista de Artes y Letras,* published an editorial on the slander in the March 1936 issue. La Liga Puertorriqueña e Hispana launched a protest campaign. A parents' organization, Los Madres y Padres Pro Niños Hispanos (Parents for Hispanic Children), campaigned for an early form of bilingual education where parents would also work in the classrooms. They did not win their demands, but their ideas would form the later basis for bilingual programs in the 1960s and 1970s.

Marcantonio, then serving his first term in Congress, made a passionate speech, printed in the *Congressional Record,* calling the report "a most slanderous attack . . . made on Puerto Rican children living in New York City." He won the votes of many Latino parents.[21]

That same year Marcantonio emerged once again as a barrio hero when Pedro Albizu Campos and other Nationalist party leaders were arrested. Everyone in the barrio by the 1930s knew the name of party founder Albizu Campos. He would spend his life in and out of jail, never giving up the independence struggle.[22] When two of the Nationalists died violently while the police held them in custody, thousands of Puerto Ricans marched through the barrio to protest and listen to another fiery Marcantonio speech. He soon became cocounsel in defense of Albizu Campos.

A few weeks later, on March 21, 1937, Palm Sunday, in Ponce, Puerto Rico, demonstrators marched toward the cathedral to attend a Te Deum mass for the murdered Nationalists. The mayor of Ponce had granted a permit for the demonstration, but American-appointed Governor Blanton Winship ordered its cancellation at the last minute. As the march began, U.S. soldiers suddenly opened fire on the assemblage. Twenty people died, and more than a hundred were wounded, including a seven-year-old girl.

In the barrio people talked day and night about the outrage. More than ten thousand infuriated Puerto Ricans marched through the streets, denouncing the "Ponce Massacre" as a crime of "imperialist America."[23] At the Park Palace hall in East Harlem, the demonstrators cheered as Vito Marcantonio and others condemned the slaughter.

Small wonder that the people of El Barrio ignored accusations that Marcantonio was a "Red." They voted for those who fought for them, including Oscar García Rivera, a Puerto Rican elected to the state assembly on an independent fusion ticket with Republican party endorsement.

During World War II, when jobs opened up in war production plants, there was not much transportation available to bring more Puerto Ricans to the United States. In the first year of the war, only thirty-nine thousand arrived, although many more wanted to come. The situation was changing politically in Puerto Rico. Luis Muñoz Marín became the leader of a new and more moderate independence party, the Popular Democratic Party (PPD). The Roosevelt administration preferred him to the more radical Albizu Campos, and appointed a New Deal liberal, Rexford G. Tugwell, as the governor of Puerto Rico. With the cooperation of the PPD and Muñoz Marín, a land reform was carried out. Unemployment dropped as sixty thousand Puerto Ricans entered the armed forces and others built military bases and an electricity system for the island.

The program continued after the war as "Operation Bootstrap." Puerto Rico began to industrialize in earnest as U.S. investors rushed to the sunny tax-free paradise to open up more than five hundred factories where thirty-five thousand Puerto Ricans, the vast majority women, worked for one-fourth the wages paid in the United States. In 1948, Muñoz Marín, his pro-independence stance now modified, became the first elected governor of Puerto Rico.[24]

In 1952, after a referendum without an independence option passed easily, Puerto Rico became the Commonwealth of Puerto Rico, "a free state in association with the United States." Nonetheless, Puerto Ricans still had very little decision-making power, and the United Nations and all Puerto Rican politicians still call the island a U.S. colony today.

Although things were much better in Puerto Rico than they had been in the 1930s, it was still impossible for many working people to make more than the barest living. No matter how many factories opened, there was not enough work to go around. Unemployment persisted.

The new PPD administration, with the full backing of the U.S. government, launched a two-pronged antipoverty program. The first, unpublicized part of the plan concentrated on the sterilization of women of childbearing age. More than one-third of Puerto Rican women were "convinced" to undergo "la operación," many believing they could reverse the procedure some day.[25]

The main public program encouraged Puerto Ricans to migrate to the United States. Air transportation made it possible for one million Puerto Ricans to migrate to the mainland over the next few years. Shortly after World War II ended, enterprising American veterans bought surplus airplanes and offered cheap flights between Puerto Rico and New York. By 1947, twenty-seven of these "wildcat" airlines offered thirty-five-dollar flights. The bargain trips ended when it was revealed that job recruiters were collecting "employment agency" fees from migrants on false pretenses and paying part of the take to the airlines. The migrants arrived in New York and discovered that there were no jobs waiting. That scandal, added to the tragedy of several of the poorly equipped planes crashing into the ocean, finally brought about an outlawing of the wildcats.

Regularly scheduled airlines filled the gap, offering a "thrift" night flight for $52.50 and a regular night flight for $64. Americans traveling to or from Puerto Rico were advised to stay away from the "thrift" flights. Not pressurized, the planes had to fly at low altitudes, unable to avoid storms, terrifying many airsick passengers during the bumpy eight-hour journey.[26]

The reaction of first-time arrivals to the "Big Apple" was less than positive. One post–World War II migrant remembered:

> *The truth is that I was disillusioned when I saw New York because I thought it would be a cleaner and prettier place and that the houses would be newer. I was disappointed to see so many slums. I thought, "PR" is much prettier than this![27]*

By the mid-1950s, with manufacturing leaving New York City, about one-fourth of the migrants traveled on to other cities, mainly Philadelphia, Chicago, and Cleveland.

The Muñoz Marín government distributed a pamphlet entitled "What is Prejudice?" to people headed for the United States, attempting to prepare them for the racism they were bound to confront and urging them to be on extra-good behavior. Included in its advice was:

> *If one Puerto Rican steals, Americans who are prejudiced say that all Puerto Ricans are thieves. If one Puerto Rican doesn't work, prejudiced Americans say all of us are lazy. If one Puerto Rican throws his garbage into the street instead of into the trash can, prejudiced Americans say that all Puerto Ricans have filthy habits. So, each mistake by a Puerto Rican in the United States is paid for by all. How? We pay, because a bad opinion of us is formed. And the result may be that they discredit us, they won't give us work, or they deny us our rights.[28]*

101

This blame-the-victim approach did little to prepare people for racism. Darker-skinned Puerto Ricans, many unable to defend themselves in the language of their attackers, learned quickly that they faced a double assault—prejudice against Latinos and severe discrimination against African Americans. Name-calling was one thing, but job and housing discrimination had a terrible economic impact, especially upon darker-skinned Puerto Ricans.

Unfortunately, some Puerto Rican families adapted to the prejudices by showing obvious preference for their lighter-skinned children. Young girls especially were often reminded to hold their lips together tightly to make them appear thinner and to straighten their hair. One scholar described the hurtful impact this had on many teenage girls:

> *When she begins to seek companionship with others who look like her (that is, black Americans), with those who will not reject her, she will hear¡ Con esa no juegues! ("Don't play with that one!")* [29]

During the cold war period, few people dared to speak out against the damaging disease called racism. One of the few who did was Congressman Marcantonio. When the postwar witch-hunt's Red-baiting didn't stop his victories at the polls, a more successful method was found. Election officials engineered his defeat in the 1950 elections by simply changing the shape of his congressional district, excluding many of his supporters and adding a section of the wealthy Upper East Side to his constituency.

On August 9, 1954, in the midst of a petition campaign to place his name on the ballot again, Marcantonio suffered a heart attack and died on a downtown sidewalk. Bystanders found a crucifix and religious medal among his possessions and summoned a priest to perform the Catholic last rites. A few days later Cardinal Francis Spellman denied him a Catholic burial.

The cardinal received hundreds of protest letters and petitions from Puerto Ricans and Italians, but he would not budge. One Italian Harlem resident later asserted, "When the church wouldn't bury Marc, many people left the church."[30] More than five thousand people crowded the sidewalk in front of the funeral home as speakers from every group in Harlem eulogized their friend. On his tombstone the words read, "Vito Marcantonio: The People's Congressman."[31]

Despite the thought control atmosphere, in 1958, Puerto Rican educator Antonia Pantoja and a group of young professionals founded the Puerto Rican Forum, Inc., in New York City. Its purpose was to help Latinos launch careers by creating new Puerto Rican institutions. Some of its leaders went on to found ASPIRA in 1961, helping Latinos go on to college and campaigning against housing and employment discrimination.[32]

By the end of the 1950s, for many Americans the economic situation was much improved. The cold war created continued defense jobs, and new technologies of the space age created still more. Almost every home in the United States, no matter how poor, had managed to acquire at least a secondhand television set. In El Barrio families watched the faces of white actors and actresses portraying the "good life," dressing and eating well, working at white collar occupations. For most of them, it was a fairy tale world made for others.

Thousands of Puerto Ricans lived in misery. As one Puerto Rican scholar described it bluntly:

> *The women were overworked and underpaid in bleak garment factories, the men usually got the dirtiest and least rewarding jobs . . . a nightmare of cold winters in unheated and roach-infested apartments . . . It was a world of unsympathetic and bigoted*

social workers and teachers, brutal policemen, broken
families, small children bitten by rats and young men
and women driven by their surroundings and
hopelessness to crime and drug addiction. [33]

Anger grew in the ghettos. As young and often unemployed Latinos sat on front stoops on hot summer days,
they started talking about the civil rights marches in the
South and what they could do to win a better life for
Puerto Ricans. They were about to take some direct action of their own and become an important part of the
exciting decade of the sixties.

5

cinco

Into
the
Streets

The civil rights movement shook America to the core. Initiated by blacks in the deep South in the mid-1950s, it affected people everywhere—from the quiet halls of Ivy League colleges to the noisy streets of urban slums. Starting in the 1960s, two opposing schools of thought emerged within the movement. One held that justice would come gradually, through use of the courts and the ballot box. The other advocated more direct action—taking to the streets for "freedom now." Later, as we shall see, another internal battle within the movement would pit women against men.

In New York City's Spanish Harlem in 1961, marchers in the street celebrated the election of Carlos Ríos as the first Puerto Rican Democratic party district leader. Mayor Robert Wagner and Eleanor Roosevelt, the widow of President Franklin Delano Roosevelt, had actually come to the neighborhood, visiting apartments where rats had chewed the furniture and toilets overflowed. Surely, parents told their children, these important people would do something.[1]

But nothing changed. The slum landlords refused to repair rotten plumbing and falling plaster, the rats and roaches continued to breed in the piles of uncollected garbage. Barrio hospitals remained markedly inferior to those in white neighborhoods. Lincoln Hospital, a crumbling building more than a century old in the South Bronx's sprawling barrio, claimed to serve half a million residents. Locals called it "the butcher shop." The schools were filled with teachers who had no respect for Spanish-speaking pupils, and the children weren't learning. Very few Latinos were able to pass admission tests to attend the city's special high schools or free colleges. The available jobs continued to be the dirtiest and lowest paying. The few Latinos who earned enough to move to a better neighborhood quickly discovered that most landlords would not rent to them.

Farm workers, the majority of them Mexicans and Mexican Americans in the Southwest, were probably the worst-off and most forgotten group in the nation. Puerto Rican, Caribbean, and African American farm workers in the East and South were also terribly oppressed. In California, farm workers met in 1962 at the first convention of a new union, the National Farm Workers Association. They elected Cesar Chavez and Dolores Huerta, among others, as their spokespeople. One of their earliest actions was to join a group of striking Filipino grape pickers in Delano, California.

At around the same time, a small group of mostly white Michigan college students announced the formation of Students for a Democratic Society (SDS). Very few people had any idea that within a few short years the farm workers' union would make headline news and SDS would be energizing a sweeping movement against the Vietnam War.

Many people were angry when civil rights worker

Medgar Evers was shot down in front of his home in Jackson, Mississippi on June 11, 1963. Millions watched Dr. Martin Luther King, Jr. on their television sets on August 28, 1963, telling a civil rights throng of more than 100,000 gathered in the nation's capitol for the "March on Washington" about his dream of equality of all races. A few months later on November 22, 1963, President John F. Kennedy was assassinated and Vice President Lyndon Baines Johnson was sworn into the presidency just hours later.

During the early summer of 1964, busloads of young people, many of them white college students, traveled down to Mississippi for a voter registration drive organized by the Student Non-Violent Coordinating Committee (SNCC). Within weeks the horrifying news came that the bodies of three missing young civil rights workers, two Jewish and one black, had been found in the swamps of Misssissippi.

Deluged by protest letters and telephone calls from all over the country, President Johnson signed the Civil Rights Act of 1964, which outlawed both segregation in public accommodations and job discrimination. Then he signed the Economic Opportunity Act, earmarking almost one billion dollars for a war on poverty.

A virtual alphabet soup of programs descended into mostly African American slums. Programs with names like Upward Bound and Neighborhood Youth Corps handled the task of training welfare mothers and other poor people for new jobs. The number of people below the all-too-low official poverty line momentarily dropped, but the visible impact was slight. To many people, the programs felt like a drop of water in a desert.

Latino neighborhoods saw very little of the antipoverty programs until angry young people of Spanish Harlem poured into the streets in a "riot" or "rebellion" in 1965. One young participant commented on the sudden arrival of the antipoverty programs after the disturbances:

*They bought out a lot of the young cats who were
leading the rebellions. A lot of dudes who were
throwing bricks one day found themselves directors of
anti-poverty programs the next, or workers on Mayor
Lindsay's Urban Action Core.*[2]

Other than some "directors" jobs in poverty programs,
however, there were few changes. Within the year, as
people grew more impatient with the go-slow reformers
who had been leading the movement for a decade, a new,
more militant movement took shape across the nation. It
started like a brushfire here and there, and ended in an
enormous conflagration of social protest.

Poor women were among the earliest to move. Despite the promised reforms, welfare mothers continued to
live in utter misery, their dignity stripped, their children
hungry. There were no jobs or affordable day-care centers. Ignored by everyone, the mothers started organizing.

Serafina L. was one of the first members of an early
welfare rights organization.[3] She and her husband had left
Puerto Rico and come to Spanish Harlem in 1950, looking for work. Chronically unemployed and desperate, her
husband disappeared in 1959. Without training or skills
of any kind and with no one to look after her children,
Serafina was forced to apply for public assistance, barely
enough to feed her small children. Worried about the
drugs and rotten schools in the barrio, she moved into an
ancient railroad flat apartment on East 14th Street. Directly across the street, she could see the middle-class
apartments of Stuyvesant Town.

Down the street lived Pepi R., a disabled Puerto
Rican veteran of World War II, barely surviving on dis-
ability checks. Pepi sometimes found broken toys in the
Stuyvesant Town garbage bins and fixed them up for
Serafina's children. Right before Christmas in 1962, he
spotted a discarded television set in the refuse, got it work-
ing with a new tube or two, and brought it over to
Serafina's apartment as a Christmas present.

The social worker in charge of Serafina's case dropped in out of the blue almost every week. She always looked in the closet to see if she could spot any men's clothing there. The day after Christmas she made one of her surprise visits. In the tiny cubicle that passed for a living room, the children were happily sprawled on the floor watching television cartoons. The social worker, according to Serafina, "acted like a crazy person." She rushed into the kitchen, where Serafina was preparing lunch, shouting and sputtering, "Where did you get the television set?" Serafina explained innocently that Pepi had given it to them for Christmas. The social worker grew even more excited. "Then you have a boyfriend supporting you! I'll have to report this! You can't take a welfare check and get money from a man!"

Serafina's checks stopped coming. Desperate, she went for help to some neighbors who were trying to form a welfare rights group. One of them went down with Serafina to the Department of Welfare and argued with a bureaucrat there. Serafina's payments were eventually restored.

By 1966, the National Welfare Rights Organization (NWRO) had pulled together thousands of Serafinas across the country. The women were tired of living in fear and having to beg for every shred of warm clothing and every morsel of food for their children. They wanted the right to have a checking account, instead of paying exorbitant fees to check-cashing agencies. They wanted to be treated with dignity.

The NWRO won many concessions, including *scheduled* visits from caseworkers and the right to a checking account. The organization helped desperate women apply for welfare and published a book combating what they termed the "welfare mythology," especially the "hard-work myth" that "assumes that everyone on welfare is able to work." They publicized the fact that almost one-quarter of the national welfare caseload were elderly; 8 percent were permanently and totally disabled; 1 percent were blind; and more than half were children. Only 13 percent were mothers, of whom a mere fifth were in job-training programs or were holding jobs that paid so little that they still qualified for aid! Only 8 percent were able-bodied men, and they had to prove they were searching for work.

NWRO criticized Johnson's job-training programs, claiming that employers benefited most. Their book provided the figures:

> *Most outrageous they subsidize the normal work*
> *force. The State Poultry Company in Jackson*
> *Mississippi had 242 employees. It received $408,190*
> *to hire 140. . . trainees with wages at $1.60 rising*
> *to $1.80. When training was over most lost their*
> *jobs.* [4]

Many Latinas were recruited into NWRO and became leaders in their own communities. Mrs. Clementina Castro, a migrant worker who came to Milwaukee looking for a better job, became vice chairman of Union Benefica Hispana Welfare Rights Organization and sergeant at arms of Milwaukee County NWRO. She pressed for the hiring of more Spanish-speaking caseworkers and a minimum standard of living for welfare families. "This is the richest country in the world and people here have a right to live decent," she said. [5]

In 1965, another movement that counted on women activists and leaders swung into action. In California, the National Farm Workers Association, renamed the United Farm Workers (UFW), launched an all-out strike against the Delano grape growers, producers of the bulk of the world's grapes.

Close by, at the University of California in Berkeley, some of the students returned to school after spending a horrifying summer in Mississippi, and they were determined to work for civil rights. They set up literature tables on the campus, publicizing the plight of African Americans. College officials quickly banned all campus political activities. The students protested this infringment on their free speech rights and held daily rallies on campus. Instead of negotiating, the administration called the police. One student leader was arrested and eight others were suspended. The Berkeley Free Speech Movement (FSM) was born. Imitating the successful labor union sit-ins of the 1930s, the students planned to occupy the administration building, Sproul Hall, on December 2, if the deans refused to meet with them.

The FSM's gender-based division of labor was apparent from the first. The women students distributed literature, ran for coffee, and listened to the speeches of the male leaders. The only woman mentioned in press releases was a celebrity who came to lend her presence on the day of the sit-in. Joan Baez, a popular young Mexican American folksinger, came to the rally, sang the anthem of the civil rights movement, "We Shall Overcome," and led the march into the administration building.

Time magazine had featured Baez on its cover in 1962. Now she was risking her career. But activism was nothing new to Baez. She had marched with Martin Luther King, Jr. in Alabama, and in 1963, long before most Americans knew where Vietnam was on the map, she had been invited to the White House and told President Johnson and his elegantly dressed guests that the United States should get out of Vietnam.[6]

By December 18, a victory at Berkeley had been won, and free speech was permitted on the campus. The UFW's Cesar Chavez visited the Berkeley campus and asked the victorious students to support a grape boycott. Hundreds of students swung into action, visiting food markets and liquor stores to urge management to refuse to carry non-union grapes and the Gallo wines made from the grapes. Otherwise, they would boycott the stores.

By 1966, the boycott was having an impact. UFW members took to the road, marching 250 miles from

111

Delano to the state capitol at Sacramento. Americans sitting in their living rooms saw ragged and exhausted men, women, and children straggling along the line of march. Thousands more refused to buy grapes. A few growers signed up with the union, but the rest held out.

Dolores Huerta, the UFW vice-chairman, was widely respected and admired throughout the Mexican American community. She preferred to keep out of the public eye, but Chavez and other insiders knew full well that the grape strike might have failed if not for Huerta's organizing and negotiating skills.

She was born Dolores Fernandez in 1930 in a mining town in New Mexico. Her mother, Alicia Chavez Fernandez, was a third-generation Mexican American and her father, Juan Fernandez, was the son of Mexican immigrants. Juan worked as a coal miner and migrant sugar-beet picker. Times were hard, and the marriage suffered. When Dolores was very young, her parents divorced, and she moved with her mother to Stockton, California. While Alicia Fernandez worked in a cannery at night and waited tables during the day, Dolores's widowed grandfather took care of the children.

In high school Dolores dreamed of being a writer. "But the teacher told me at the end of the year that she couldn't give me an A because she knew that somebody was writing my papers for me," she later remembered.[7]

In the early 1950s, Dolores's mother remarried, and things became financially easier. Dolores enrolled at Stockton College, but marriage and the birth of two daughters ended her studies. A few years later, her marriage ended, and Dolores returned to school, counting on her mother to watch over her children. She planned to teach, but during her training she realized "that as a teacher I couldn't do anything for the kids who came to school barefoot and hungry."[8]

She married Ventura Huerta, a community activist, and became an organizer for the Community Service Organization, where Cesar Chavez also worked. Dolores Huerta developed into a skilled lobbyist for Mexican farm workers.

In 1962, when Huerta began organizing farm workers with Chavez, she was pregnant with her seventh child. Like so many working women, she tried to juggle her activities, pushing herself to the limit around the clock to keep up with three "jobs": paid work, housework, and community activism. Sometimes she felt overwhelmed and guilty: "I had serious doubts whether I was doing the right thing, giving kids a lousy supper to go to a council meeting," she told an interviewer. "I didn't come out and tell my husband that I cared more about helping other people than cleaning our house and doing my hair."[9] Huerta's marriage crumbled, but she continued to make the cause of the farm workers the most important thing in her life.

Always modest about her own role, Huerta praised the other women active in the UFW. She was proud that the union treated them as equal decision makers along with the men. Day care for the children was provided, and no married man went out on the picket lines unless his wife also came. Huerta said this was only right. "Women had picked, pruned and packed in fields, cannery and shed side by side with men."[10]

That was not the situation women encountered in the civil rights movement or the student wing of the antiwar movement. In the Student Nonviolent Coordinating Committee (SNCC), black women were in every bit as much danger from racist violence as the men. Nevertheless, when the women asked for decision-making positions in the organization, one of the top leaders, Stokeley Carmichael, commented that "The only position for women in SNCC is prone."[11] Some members were shocked at this "joke," but Carmichael remained in the leadership and women kept making coffee and cleaning up headquarters.

The same situation prevailed in SDS, where women

members cooked, clerked, and were generally considered sex objects for the male leadership. At the December 1965 national SDS convention, when some of the women submitted a statement supporting women's liberation, they were told they were taking attention away from the Vietnam War. When they persisted in their demands, they were pelted with tomatoes and tossed out of the meeting hall. The situation grew only worse. Marilyn Salzman-Webb made a speech on women's rights at a demonstration during President Richard Nixon's inauguration in 1969. Men in the audience booed and shouted out sexist remarks.[12]

Dolores Huerta explained why she believed there were such glaring differences between the UFW's treatment of women and the behavior of these other organizations.

> *Excluding women, protecting them, keeping women at home, that's the middle-class way. Poor people's movements have always had whole families on the line, ready to move at a moment's notice, with more courage because that's all we had. It's a class not an ethnic thing.[13]*

Huerta believed that excluding women from leadership roles deprived the movements of an enormous pool of talent.

> *I think women are particularly good negotiators because we have a lot of patience, and no big ego trips to overcome. Women are more tenacious and that helps a great deal. It unnerves the growers to negotiate with us. Cesar always wanted to have an* all-woman *negotiating team.[14]*

The all-male Young Lords group was born in Chicago in 1966, where only little more than thirty-two thousand Puerto Ricans lived. Latinos there had remained calm under the influence of a church organization, Los Caballeros de San Juan.[15] Los Caballeros emphasized self-improvement and "Americanization" but had little impact on the severe economic problems afflicting Chicago's Puerto Rican community. Antipoverty programs were even less effective in Chicago than in other cities. Mayor Richard Daley used the programs to increase his own influence, hiring his cronies to fill most of the poverty-program jobs. The situation changed on June 12, 1966, when a white policeman shot and wounded a twenty-year-old Puerto Rican man. As Division Street, the main barrio thoroughfare, filled with protestors, police dogs attacked them, and a man was bitten. Most had seen the television news broadcasts of Southern sheriffs' dogs in Mississippi mauling black civil rights demonstrators. The crowds quickly swelled to more than three thousand, and for three days and nights they refused to leave the area. Rocks were thrown and stores were looted and burned. When calm was restored on June 15, sixteen people had been hurt, 49 arrested, and over 50 buildings destroyed.

Many people, especially the youth, began to question the effectiveness of the old-style leadership. Los Caballeros had nothing to say when the Chicago Police Department set up a political surveillance unit to spy on every activist and organization in the barrio. Soon after the Division Street riots, the city government expanded its urban renewal projects in the barrio and pushed Puerto Rican families out of their homes to make way for upscale white professionals. Many people asked, "Why should we have to keep moving while other people stay?"[16]

The minister of the Armitage Street Methodist Church had been working with street gangs for years. He convinced a 3,000-member gang called the Latin Kings to work on the urban renewal issue. Renaming themselves the Young Lords, they occupied the buildings of the McCormick Theological Seminary for almost a week, publicizing the planned eviction of the area's Puerto Ricans. They managed to make peace between black, white, and Latino street gangs, even forming a coalition with the Black Panther Party and a white gang, the Young Patriots Organization.

Despite harassment by city officials and the police, the Young Lords opened a day-care center in the basement of the Armitage Avenue church in the summer of 1969, and also ran a health clinic with volunteer medical personnel. Initially, women were afraid to go, remembering the old tough Latin Kings with less than fondness. But health workers campaigned door-to-door, and soon the clinic was filled with patients. Women were not invited to join Chicago's Young Lords, although they worked in the day-care center and kitchen and were harassed by the police for working with the men.

At first, only a few isolated Latino college students were active in the civil rights movement and the emerging student movement. Small groups of Latino students urged college administrators to recruit Latino students and provide tutorial programs to help them make the transition from their substandard high schools to college. Maria Varela cofounded an SDS chapter at the University of Michigan and later helped establish an adult literacy program in Alabama. Elizabeth Sutherland Martinez was director of the New York City SNCC in 1964 and spent time in Mississippi. Both women quickly realized that black Americans, immersed in their own difficult struggle, had little knowledge or concern about Latinos.

In the Southwest and Midwest, poverty programs ignored poor Mexicans. Middle-class Mexican Americans had organized Viva Kennedy Clubs in the Southwest to help elect John F. Kennedy in 1960. They were hurt and upset when the Democratic party declined to support Mexican American candidates for statewide office. Under pressure from them, the Johnson administration created

116

a Mexican American committee with no real power. In 1966, LULAC and other respected Mexican American civil rights male leaders attended a conference called by the federal Equal Employment Commission in Albuquerque, New Mexico. The civil rights leaders complained about this exclusionary policy of the poverty programs. After being ignored for an hour, they walked out together. One of them, Rodolfo "Corky" Gonzalez, formed the Crusade for Justice and emerged as the leader of a new "Chicano" movement. Young Mexican Americans began calling themselves "Chicano"—a term traditionally used by working-class elements to describe themselves and by more affluent Mexican Americans to put them down.[17]

Although many Chicano students admired Chavez, most of them lived in cities by then and wanted to address the problems of urban slums. The Crusade for Justice became their rallying point. Gonzalez, a Presbyterian leader, poet and former boxer, became the central figure in the organization.[18] Rejecting the "hat-in-hand" approach of begging those in power for crumbs, the Crusade launched demonstrations in the streets against discrimination and the Vietnam War.[19]

For a while older Mexican Americans moved into the limelight—Chavez and Huerta, Gonzalez and a Bible-thumping preacher named Reis Lopez Tijerina. Citing the 1848 Treaty of Guadalupe Hidalgo as legal justification, Tijerina launched a struggle in New Mexico using both the courts and the tactics of the old "social bandits" of the Southwest to win back the land taken from Mexicans after the U.S.-Mexico War. He was thrown into jail.

By the end of 1967, Chicano students occasionally joined in antiwar protests but usually concentrated on educational issues. They brought Chavez, Tijerina, and Gonzalez to speak on campuses, collected food for the Delano farm workers, and joined the picket lines in front of supermarkets in support of the grape boycott. But they seemed very quiet compared with the SDS students who were in the limelight all over the country.

Around that time, Mexican American gangs in East Los Angeles transformed themselves into political groups. These young Chicano militants marched on the streets, calling themselves Brown Berets (and wearing them). They protested police brutality and racism in the schools, published a newspaper, and opened a free clinic. All over the Southwest similar groups popped up spontaneously.

In New Mexico in October 1967, Tijerina, temporarily out of jail, organized a conference for the formation of a new political party, La Raza Unida (United Race). Young Chicanos called the meeting "the last chance you older Chicanos have to come through. If nothing happens from this you'll have to step aside—or we'll walk over you."[20]

La Raza Unida's platform called for job-training programs, rights for farm workers, redistribution of wealth, and condemnation of the Vietnam War. Women were admitted to membership, but they were not permitted to work on feminist issues. Combating racism was considered more central to the struggle for women's equality than any battle against sexism.

That year several other new organizations cropped up, including the United Mexican American Students (UMAS) and the Mexican American Youth Organization (MAYO). All of them rejected the traditional go-slow strategies of political and court action.

La Raza Unida candidates gained control of the city council and board of education in the 1970 elections in Crystal City, Texas. Later, speakers at conferences proudly proclaimed that women were active participants in the party, comprising 15 percent of the candidates for state office.[21]

While he was in Memphis in 1968 to help striking sanitation workers, Martin Luther King, Jr. was shot by a white assassin. African Americans rioted in 168 cities. Living in nearby slums, many equally frustrated young Latinos joined them. The impact of Dr. King's death and the escalating war in Vietnam had an effect on high-school students, who would be eligible for the draft as soon as they graduated. They wanted the right to discuss the war in school. In some districts, principals gave permission for all-day teach-ins on the subject. In East Los Angeles, this was not the case.

On the morning of March 3, 1968, over a thousand Mexican American students, led by their teachers, walked out of Abraham Lincoln High School in East Los Angeles. Their cries of "Blow Out!" rang through the halls. Outside they linked up with other activists and demonstrated with signs calling for free speech, the hiring of more Latino teachers, and courses in Mexican American culture and history. At five other barrio schools, thousands of others left classrooms and joined them.

The day after the student strike started, FBI director J. Edgar Hoover ordered law enforcement agencies to investigate the "Brown Power" strike in East Los Angeles. In early June, thirteen strike leaders were indicted by the Los Angeles County grand jury on conspiracy charges. The new movement continued to grow despite an aggressive government campaign against it.[22]

During all of 1968 and into 1969, the different wings of the now many movements spread, occasionally linking up for massive antiwar marches. Across the ocean in Europe and across the border in Mexico, students demonstrated against the Vietnam War. In Paris ten million workers joined the students and called a general strike that shut the city down. It was the time of massive Vietnamese offensives to drive the Americans out.[23]

In March 1969, at the height of all the activity, the Crusade for Justice called a National Chicano Youth Liberation Conference in Denver to bring together representatives of all of the diverse groups. More than a thousand people attended.

Enriqueta Longauex y Vasquez, writing later about the beginning of Chicana feminism, remembered the conference vividly. A workshop was held on the role of women. Most of the women felt more discussion was needed to sort out all their feelings. When the full conference reconvened, a spokesperson for the women's workshop reported: "It was the consensus of the group that the Chicana woman does not want to be liberated." Later, several shocked and angry Chicanas protested and formed campus groups and other workshops at conferences to continue their discussions. The subject was not going to disappear.[24]

A month later at another conference in Santa Barbara, California, El Movimiento Estudiantil Chicano de Aztlan (MECHA) was formed. The new organization, dedicated to *Chicanismo* (Chicano nationalism), resolved to engage in a massive membership drive. One Chicana later described the attitudes toward women who were interested in the organization:

> *When a freshman male comes to MECHA . . . he is approached and welcomed. He is taught by observation that the Chicanas are only useful in areas of clerical and sexual activities. When something must be done there is always a Chicana there to do the work.*[25]

Throughout all the student movements women complained that they performed menial labor and played no real role in the leadership. Chicanas, aware of the racism that affected all Latinos, softened their pleas for equality in order to keep the emphasis on combating racism. Some of them also appreciated the fact that Chicanos had never treated them in the rude and disrespectful way the whites had treated SNCC and SDS women.

A statement issued by Chicana women of the Brown Women's Venceremos Collective illustrates how Chicanas tried to keep the issue of women's equality alive without disrupting activities.

> *Venceremos supports no separatist movements on any level. While at the same time recognizing the initial importance of the women's struggle, the success of the revolution, of our fight to eliminate political, economic and social injustices will depend on equal efforts. Women are one half and the men the other half. Neither can win without the other. . . . There is no place for male chauvinism. Women should be strong and men need to respect their strength, and should not try to force them back into weaker roles.*[26]

Contrary to the super-chauvinist *"macho"* myth about Latinos, the first Latino group to officially condemn male chauvinism shortly after its formation was the Young Lords Party in New York City. In May 1969, a handful of Puerto Rican college students met to discuss how to organize Puerto Ricans in New York City. Before long, a Young Lords group existed on the Lower East Side in Manhattan, affiliated with the Chicago organization.

The New Yorkers engaged in even more ambitious programs than Chicago's Young Lords. They supported welfare mothers' groups, organized hospital workers, and embarked on free breakfast and lead poisoning detection programs. "We attacked police for allowing drug traffic to come into the neighborhood, and then busting junkies instead of the big pushers," one Young Lords leader recalled. They broadcast a weekly radio program, published a newspaper, and organized new party branches in the South Bronx and Spanish Harlem. Later in 1969 they decided to form an independent political party, the Young Lords Party, open to women and men agreeing with their program.[27]

When the minister of Spanish Harlem's First Spanish Methodist Church refused to open the church basement for a free breakfast program, Young Lords representatives came to the church on December 7 to speak directly to the congregation. The minister called the police. During the battle that followed, women fought back alongside the men and were among the thirteen who were beaten and arrested.

Party leaders described this event as the beginning of a head-on fight against sexism. The final version of their program called for full equality for women, stating that the "doctrine of machismo has been used by men to take out their frustration on wives, sisters, mothers, and children."[28]

On December 28, 1969, the Young Lords armed themselves and returned to the church, barricading the door and occupying it for eleven days. They distributed clothing, provided free breakfasts and dinners, health services, ran a day-care center, a "liberation school," and showed films in the evening. Over 100,000 people from the barrio participated. They called it the "People's Church." On January 7, police battered down the door and arrested the known leaders of the Young Lords Party, charging them with civil contempt. Strong community support led to the dropping of all charges in March.

With New York City a hubbub of activism in the late 1960s, Dolores Huerta went east and organized a ground swell of support for the grape boycott. The following year, the growers signed the first decent contracts ever given to farm workers. Once again, Dolores Huerta was modest about her achievement:

> *When Cesar first sent me to New York on the boycott it was the first time we'd done anything like that. I thought, 11 million people in New York, and I have to persuade them to stop buying grapes. Well, I didn't do it alone. When you need people, they come to you. You find a way. . . it gets easier all the time.*[29]

Since women did most of the family shopping, Huerta counted on them as her most active supporters. She contacted Gloria Steinem, a leader in the National Organization of Women (NOW), and soon there was considerable publicity for the boycott. Huerta also received her first exposure to middle-class feminists and developed ties with their predominantly white women's movement.

NOW was the largest group in the women's liberation movement. It had been organized in 1966 by professional women, but since then other groups had mushroomed in many cities. Most of the members were younger veterans of other movements, tired of having their concerns ridiculed.

In May 1970, when the nation learned that Richard Nixon had extended the Vietnam War into Cambodia despite his election promises to end the war, antiwar activity reached a fever pitch. Unarmed white students at Kent State and black students at Jackson State were fired upon by National Guardsmen, and several were killed. Student strikes on college and high-school campuses all over the nation closed down many universities. Students held classes to discuss the issues of the day instead of the assigned curriculum. Young Lords, Black Panthers, women's groups and student groups rallied and marched together.

On August 26, 1970, a coalition of NOW and other feminist groups commemorated the fiftieth anniversary of women's suffrage with rallies and marches in several cities. In New York, twenty thousand women marched down Fifth Avenue, calling for child-care centers, abortion rights, and equal opportunity in education and jobs.[30]

The East Coast Regional Central Committee of the Young Lords met to decide on future activities. Moved by all of the feminist activism in New York City, they placed the "woman question" high on their agenda. According to a spokesperson:

One of the main areas that we attacked was
machismo and male chauvinism. . . . The attitudes
of superiority that brothers had toward sisters would
have to change. . . .[31]

Women like Denise Oliver and Gloria Gonzalez already
were Young Lords leaders. Denise, a black Puerto Rican,
was raised in a middle-class family and had briefly attended the State University at Old Westbury, Long Island.
Impatient to do something for her people, she had quit
school, moved to the barrio, and worked for an antipoverty program. Disillusioned by the program, she joined the
Young Lords Party in October 1969. In March 1971, remaining on good terms with the Young Lords, she joined
the Black Panther party.

Gloria Gonzalez had been born in Puerto Rico and
actively supported the independence cause in her country. A junior high-school dropout, she took a job as a
health worker in a Bronx hospital when she came to the
United States, and helped start an activist organization in
her workplace. In February 1970, after the People's
Church occupation, she joined the Young Lords Party.

In July 1970 the Young Lords occupied decrepit Lincoln Hospital. The hospital's chief administrator, Dr.
Antero Lacot, told the press that the Lords had helped
the community by dramatizing intolerable conditions at
the facility. As a result of the publicity, more Puerto
Ricans were added to the staff, including Dr. Helen
Rodriguez, named as chief of pediatrics (see chapter 6).

All through the rest of 1970, the Young Lords were
active in the antiwar movement and continued their community work. In Newark, New Jersey and Philadelphia,
new branches were organized, with women as full and active members. Perhaps taking a cue from the Young Lords
Party, a Chicano group in the Southwest, Las Gorras Ne-
gras (Black Berets), recognized "that our women are
equals within our struggle for liberation."[32]

Repression followed closely on the heels of the Young Lords' success. The Philadelphia branch was firebombed. Then, on October 15, Young Lords activist Julio Roldan, arrested and held in the Manhattan Men's Prison, the notorious "Tombs," was found hanging in his cell. For years Puerto Ricans and blacks had been "committing suicide" under highly improbable circumstances. Two thousand people marched through the streets of El Barrio on October 18 to protest Roldan's death.

After the May 1970 student strikes against the Vietnam War, with majority public opinion turning against the war, the Nixon administration began to withdraw American soldiers from Vietnam. The last huge antiwar demonstrations took place in 1970. On August 29, thousands of Chicanos gathered in Laguna Park in East Los Angeles for a rally and march during a Chicano moratorium against the Vietnam War. Police suddenly attacked the gathering, wounding many people and killing three, including television news reporter Rubén Salazar.[33]

Three years later, when Richard Nixon resigned from the presidency rather than be impeached, many closely guarded secrets leaked out. It was revealed that as early as 1956, the beginning of the civil rights movement, the FBI ran a program known as COINTELPRO, short for Counter Intelligence Program, to disrupt and destroy the movement. When protest activities grew instead, the Nixon administration expanded its scandalous violation of civil liberties. Telephones and homes were wiretapped, drugs were planted in activists' cars and homes, and police and federal agents pretending to be loyal members of Latino, African American, antiwar, and women's organizations acted as provocateurs. They attempted to provoke members into illegal actions that even led to the murder of Black Panther leaders in Chicago.[34]

A special and highly effective part of the program of disruption aimed at Puerto Rican organizations was called "Operation Chaos." A Young Lords leader later described its impact: "Many left the ranks . . . cynicism and mistrust set in."[35] The Brown Berets in Los Angeles dissolved their organization in late 1972. They told the press that too many problems had been created by police informants posing as members.[36]

The women's liberation movement in the early 1970s centered its activity around a popular cause: legal, safe abortion. In 1973, after a state-by-state campaign of marches, lobbying, public meetings and court cases, the Supreme Court decision in *Roe v. Wade* legalized abortion. It was a tremendous victory for all women, but even more so for the poor. Well-off women had been able to travel to countries where abortion was legal or pay a high fee to a doctor for a safe procedure performed in secret. Poor women had no such choices, and many had died at the hands of low-priced, untrained abortionists. After legalization, federal programs like Medicaid funded abortion services for women who could not afford to pay.

Very few Chicanas in the Southwest and Puertorriqueñas on the East Coast were part of the women's liberation movement. Latinas wanted the same things other women wanted—day care, an end to sex discrimination, birth control information, and legal abortion. But many believed that white women were oblivious to the problems of racism and poverty. Latinas wanted *bilingual* and *bicultural* child care so that their children would not forget the language and culture of their parents and would learn English faster.

"Minority women could fill volumes with examples of put-downs, put-ons, and out-and-out racism shown to them by the leadership of the movement," claimed Marta Cotera, an activist scholar. When clerical women workers went on strike at Barnard College in 1974, "the strikers waited in vain for support from feminist professors." Latinas and others struggling to support their families as clerks, seamstresses, and factory workers, felt that the

"Vassar, Wellesley and Radcliffe graduates who control so much of the movement," looked down on them.[37]

Some Latinas stayed away from the women's movement because they believed it was antimale, antifamily, and too sexually free. Others remained aloof because they believed that the main issue was human rights for men and women. But many Chicana feminists believed that they needed *both* a strong civil rights movement *and* a strong Latina feminist movement.

In 1971, Chicanas met at a conference in Houston, Texas. Two factions emerged. One claimed that Chicanas were oppressed because all Chicanos suffered from oppression and echoed the men's claim that feminism was an Anglo diversion. Others presented a more feminist position. "The issue of equality, freedom and self-determination of the Chicana," they insisted, "is not negotiable."[38]

Some Latinas, most of them college students, formed their own feminist organizations—the Hijas de Cuauhtémoc, the Comisión Femenil Mexicana, and the Chicana Service Action Center for employment and job training. In 1973 the first Chicana journal, *Encuentro Femenil,* was founded by Adalaida del Castillo and edited by Anna Nieto-Gómez.[39] The issues of medical experimentation, sterilization without a woman's consent, and legal abortion for poor women had been largely ignored by mainstream feminists. They became important concerns for Latina feminists.

For years Latinas, especially women in Puerto Rico, had been used as experimental subjects in drug studies. In 1957, during a birth control–pill test, five women died after suffering symptoms suggestive of blood clots. No autopsies were performed. Although there was every reason to suspect that the pill might have contributed to the deaths, the new "wonder" contraceptive was declared *safe* and brought into wide use in Puerto Rico and the United States.[40] By 1975, George Washington University Medical Center in St. Louis announced that women taking "the pill" ran a far greater risk of suffering a stroke or heart attack, as well as certain forms of cancer.[41]

The Comisión Femenil backed a civil suit against a Los Angeles hospital for allegedly allowing the sterilization of nonconsenting Chicana women between 1971 and 1974. The medical personnel discussing the procedure with the women were not Spanish-speaking, and many of the women had gone into surgery not realizing that they would never be able to have children again. The judge cleared the hospital of blame. In his decision he stated, "One can sympathize with them [the sterilized women] for their inability to communicate clearly, but one can hardly blame the doctors for relying on these indicia of consent."[42]

Then, on August 1, 1977, Congress passed the Hyde Amendment, prohibiting federal payments for abortions. Latinas considered this an important test of the sincerity of Anglo feminists. The old problem had returned. Poor women were accused of having too many babies but were barred from access to safe ways of terminating unwanted pregnancies. There was a mild flurry of protest from the women's movement, but no massive protest campaign to protect less fortunate women.[43]

There were sporadic efforts throughout the 1970s to revive the movements of the 1960s. At a statewide conference at the California State University at Northridge, for example, in December 1972, attempts were initiated to revive MECHA. Resolutions were passed affirming an equal role for women in the leadership of the student movement.[44] Similar efforts were made by Latinas to reinvigorate La Raza Unida in 1975. Chicanas formed a group called La Federación de Mujeres del Partido Raza Unida in Southern California. They called for leadership roles for women, tempering their remarks by saying, "Our struggle is not a battle of the sexes but a common struggle for the true liberation alongside the men."[45] But everyone seemed to know that they were really saying a belated farewell to the sixties. Nothing much came of either effort.

Local activists won some victories when they concentrated on more pressing issues. In the Division Street neighborhood of Chicago, a new movement against "urban removal" sprang up after mysterious fires swept through the area. Many community activists believed the fires were part of an organized plot to get rid of Latinos in order to open up the area for middle-class buyers. On July 17, 1976, a sweeping fire took the lives of five children and two adults. Eight hundred people crammed into the local high school for hearings on the problem and then met with city officials. In an article headlined "Torches: Arson for Sale" in *Newsweek* on Sept 12, 1977, more than a year later, Terry Atlas exposed the arsonists' motivations:

> *A great many deliberate fires, perhaps the majority, are the work of the arson industry—a shadow world of property owners, mortgage men, corrupt fire officials, insurance adjusters and mobsters.*

Activists won a partial victory when a program was established for the rehabilitation of a few buildings to be sold or rented to low- and moderate-income families.[46]

Unified Latino organizations also addressed the problem of growing unemployment. In 1971 Chicanos and Puerto Ricans in Chicago formed the Spanish Coalition for Jobs and also the Latino Institute. Some jobs were won under federal affirmative action programs forcing employers receiving funds from the government to hire minority workers as required by the 1964 Civil Rights Act.[47]

The militant movements of the 1960s had won gains that could never be completely reversed. Soon, those noisy and active days were long gone, as everyone scrambled to earn a living and survive the budgetary cutbacks of the late

1970s and the severely deteriorating economy of the 1980s and early 1990s.

Nevetheless, Latino teachers, both women and men, were being hired, and bilingual programs were being introduced. Hostos Community College had been founded in 1969 in the South Bronx, with Cándido de León as the first Puerto Rican college president in the United States, and young militants had kept its doors open every time cutbacks threatened its demise. Open admissions programs had been introduced on college campuses, and young Latino and African American students were graduating and going on to professional jobs.[48] Many people believed that there was no way for a complete rollback to take place without the probability of another, and perhaps stronger, movement emerging.

6
seis

The
Haves
and the
Have-Nots

For decades, medical schools, law schools, and most colleges were the province of white males.[1] Only an occasional white woman was accepted, and even less often, a black or Latino of either sex. In the offices of publishing companies, insurance firms, banks, and other business enterprises, African American and Latino white collar employees were rarely seen. In restaurants and hospitals, they were usually the busboys, dishwashers, orderlies, and nurses' aides. On television and in the movies, darker-skinned people occasionally appeared in bit parts as servants or as comedians' sidekicks.

The 1964 Civil Rights Act held the promise of changing that situation by outlawing employment discrimination based on race, ethnicity, or gender. The Equal Employment Opportunity Commission (EEOC) was assigned the task of "investigating" violations of the new law.

Several years passed with only slow progress.[2] As it became obvious that few employers would obey the law without a firm push, class action suits representing minorities and women and backed by civil rights groups were brought before the courts. After years of litigation, Supreme Court decisions supported the civil rights legislation. A Presidential Executive Order in 1972 ordered employers to "recruit, employ and promote" qualified people who had been formerly excluded. Although critics charged that these "affirmative action" programs were actually quota systems, supporters argued that for years there had been reverse quotas—no minorities allowed. The purpose of the new policies, they said, was to begin to play "catch-up."

With the job market finally opening up for them, Latinos tried to gain admission to college. Since high schools in poor neighborhoods were inferior, it was still very difficult to score high on college entrance examinations. Fewer than half of all Latinas graduated from high school, and in some inner city neighborhoods, the high-school dropout rates zoomed as high as 75 percent. Money for college tuition and expenses was also as scarce as ever.[3]

By the 1990s, in the five states with the most Latinos, only 7 percent held college degrees. Nationally, Latinos were only 5.5 percent of college students. More than half attended low-tuition two-year junior colleges, and dropout rates were high, but still, this was progress, however slow.[4]

The handful of college graduates naturally found better jobs than other Latinos, although frequently they were the only Hispanics in the company or one among very few "token" women and minority employees. Some firms claimed they had complied with the new laws by pointing to one employee who fulfilled all of the categories of affirmative action. A dark-skinned Latina was their "black, Hispanic female"!

Training for professions such as medicine, law, science, and engineering entailed not only four years of college but also the financing and grades to go on to graduate studies. Not suprisingly, by 1990, Latinos comprised 10.4 percent of the nation's overall labor force but only 1.6 to 5.9 percent of its professionals.[5] Census data also revealed that with the economic decline since the 1980s, the modest gains of Latinos had actually declined![6]

Progress in the professions for Latinas was especially slow. Before affirmative action, even Anglo women with high grades and money in hand were frequently excluded from law, medicine, the sciences, engineering, and college teaching—all considered "male" occupations. Traditionally, they were expected to become teachers or perhaps nurses or dietitians. But even in these so-called female professions, Latinas were hard to find. Of almost 2 million registered female nurses in the United States, only a dismally small number of 48,000 were Latinas, about 2.5 percent of the total.[7] The situation was no better in law than in medicine and far worse in science and engineering.[8]

Due to the experience of discrimination, the roughly 12,000 Latina doctors and lawyers have an outstanding record of continued concern for less fortunate Latinos. Many successful Latinas recognize special individuals— usually their mothers—as the reason for their ability to overcome the odds. Quite a few of the new Latina professionals were involved in the civil rights struggles of the 1960s and 1970s. Many Latina attorneys, for example, work for federal agencies or nonprofit civil rights and immigrant defense groups as advocates for poorer Latinos.[9]

Antonia Hernández was born in the Mexican state of Coahuila in 1948 and came to the East Los Angeles barrio with her poor immigrant parents when she was eight. There were no bilingual programs in the schools, and it was a hard upward struggle for Antonia to learn English. "I made it," she says. "But just because I made it cannot be used as an example that it works."[10] She chose law over teaching because "we couldn't help the kids as teachers unless we did something about the laws that were holding them back." A specialist in immigration and human-rights law, in 1981 she became a staff attorney for the Mexican American Legal Defense Fund (MALDEF), promoting affirmative action programs.

Dolores Atencio, president of the Hispanic National Bar Association, is one of the nation's best-known Latina attorneys. Under her leadership, HNBA has successfully lobbied the Federal Senate Judiciary to consider more Hispanic judges for appointments to the federal bench.

Atencio has commented that she had "every reason to fail." Her dark-skinned mother worked at menial jobs for low pay and urged her to follow her dream and perhaps some day make a difference in the lives of poor Latinas. She has done just that.

In 1993, the Puerto Rican Legal Defense and Education Fund commented that in New York "Latinos represent 1.7 percent of all the state's judiciary even though we represent 12 percent of the population."[11] Nationally, only 298 Latina lawyers have been appointed or elected as judges. Most have never lost sight of their roots in the Latino communities.

Irma Vidal Santaella was the first Puerto Rican woman to become a lawyer in New York State and in 1983 became the first Puerto Rican judge on the New York Supreme Court. Born in New York City in 1924, she worked her way through school in Puerto Rico and the United States, graduating from Brooklyn Law School in 1961. Santaella practiced law in the South Bronx, defending the rights of minorities and children. She helped draft an amendment to the Voting Rights Act of 1965 that eliminated English literacy tests for non-English-speaking American citizens, and in 1976 was one of the founders of the National Association for Puerto Rican Civil Rights. Het rulings are known for their strong opposition to infringements of minority rights.

Lina S. Rodriguez, born in Utah in 1949, was appointed superior court judge in Arizona in 1984. A copper miner's daughter, she is the first college graduate in her family. She credits one teacher with inspiring her in eleventh grade.

Not all teachers are so encouraging to Latinas. When Mexican American Petra Jimenez Maes told her shorthand teacher that she was interested in becoming a lawyer, she was told to become a legal secretary instead. Jimenez Maes's mother heard about this; from then on, as Petra moved closer to her goal, Mrs. Jimenez never forgot to let the shorthand teacher hear about it. Petra Jimenez Maes opened a small law office in Albuquerque and provided free legal services to New Mexico's poor. Appointed to fill a state district court vacancy in 1981, Jimenez Maes was elected for a new term and in 1984 established New Mexico's first family court. Her work to develop programs to overcome the difficulties of young people has won her MALDEF's Distinguished Service Award.

Myrna Milan, the first Hispanic woman appointed as a municipal court judge in Newark, New Jersey, is well known for developing alternative sentences for young offenders. "The goal has got to be to rehabilitate, not just penalize," she insists. Growing up in the late 1960s in nearby Hoboken, New Jersey, she took an interest in social issues when her parents held meetings in their living room on the problems faced by Latinos.

Carmen Beauchamp Ciparick, the daughter of Puerto Rican immigrants, is the first woman appointed to New York State's highest federal court—the Court of Appeals—in 1993. In a landmark decision as state Supreme Court judge in 1990, she ruled that a state program to provide prenatal care for the working poor was unconstitutional because it excluded abortions.[12]

Both Presidents George Bush and Bill Clinton have appointed Latinos as federal officials, including a few women, but less than one percent of *elected* officials nationally are Latinos. Almost all are male. Only ten are currently members of Congress.[13] In 1989, Ileana Ros-Lehtinen, a Florida Republican, became the first Latina ever elected to Congress.

Latinas are better represented at the city and county level, where they have often been in the news for their courageous performances. Gloria Molina, daughter of Mexican immigrants, is the first Latina ever to be elected to the California state legislature, the Los Angeles City Council and the Los Angeles County Board of Supervisors. Active in the Chicano movement of the 1960s and founding president of the Comisión Femenil de Los Angeles, she has long helped to develop programs for Chicanas. Before she was twenty (in 1967) she became the full-time provider for her family after her father suffered an accident. Somehow she managed to graduate from California State University in Los Angeles and remain active in community affairs. *Hispanic* magazine in July 1991 featured Molina in their cover story, describing her as a "confrontational fighter." Bill Clinton appointed her as co-chairperson of his national presidential campaign in 1992.

Another Latina featured on the cover of *Hispanic* magazine, this time in May 1992, was Miriam Santos, the daughter of Mexican immigrants, who "took on Daley in Chicago and won." In 1989, Santos was appointed city treasurer in the administration of Mayor Richard M. Daley. She was the first woman and first Hispanic to hold that post. When she embarked on a daring campaign to expose corruption in the Chicago treasury, political pundits said at the time that she may have put her political career in jeopardy unless she made peace with Daley. Santos would not give in. In 1991 she was elected treasurer, as voters gave her a higher percentage of the vote than Mayor Daley.

Latina physicians also have an outstanding record of public service. Says Catalina Esperanza Garcia, the first Latina to graduate from the University of Texas Medical School (1969): "Since there are so few Hispanic women physicians, I represent my gender and people wherever I go." Along with her busy career as a leading anesthesiologist, Garcia crusades for equal pay for equal work and raises money for women's shelters.

Dr. Helen Rodriguez, who was brought into Lincoln Hospital in the Bronx to head the Department of Pediatrics when the Young Lords Party protested the lack of Latino physicians at that facility (see chapter 5), was born in New York City in 1929 but spent most of her early years in Puerto Rico, where her Venezuelan grandparents migrated in the 1860s. She graduated from the University of Puerto Rico Medical School in 1960, specializing in pediatrics. Disturbed by the wide gap between health care for the rich and for the poor, in 1974 she went to work for St. Lukes—Roosevelt Hospital Center in New York, where she fought for more bilingual social workers and found most of her white colleagues unfriendly. "Racism is the hardest nut to crack in this country," she says. She became deeply involved in efforts to stop nonconsenting sterilization of Latinas and sexual abuse of children, lecturing on these subjects throughout the country. More recently Dr. Rodriguez has concentrated on the AIDS struggle, a mounting scourge in Puerto Rican communities. In the United States, Latinas account for over 21 percent of AIDS cases.[14] Some Latinas contract AIDS through drug abuse, but many (perhaps most) are infected by husbands or sexual partners who (as with most men) control the women's sex lives. Thus, they do not dare to urge their companions to practice "safe sex." The Coalition for Hispanic Family Services has been deeply involved in this issue as well.[15]

In the field of education, Latinas have made major contributions. There are almost two and a half million female elementary school teachers in the United States. Only 105,000 are Hispanic, but they have been crucial in the development of bilingual education. About twelve thousand Latinas teach in the nation's high schools. Many of them point out that without the bilingual programs in elementary schools, high-school dropout rates of Hispanic students would be even more horrendous.

María E. Sánchez, born in Puerto Rico in 1927, was one of a handful of pioneers in the 1960s who developed the first programs for non-English-speaking pupils. Graduating from the University of Puerto Rico in 1952, she was unable to land a job in New York City schools because of her "accent." She became an "auxiliary teacher" instead, counseling new students. She organized the Society of Puerto Rican Auxiliary Teachers and fought for licensing—"and that was the beginning of bilingual education," she says. After passage of the 1968 Bilingual Education Act, she helped establish the first bilingual kindergartens. In 1972, she developed a bilingual education major for teacher trainees at Brooklyn College, the first such undergraduate program, and became chair of the first Puerto Rican studies department created in the City University of New York, at Brooklyn College.

Elementary school teacher Rita Esquivel played a similar pioneering role in California. She was the first person in her Mexican American family to graduate from high school. From 1989 through 1992 she headed the office of Bilingual Education and Minority Language Affairs of the U.S. Department of Education, expanding bilingual programs and establishing scholarships for Latinos. Since then she has been the first female director of the Adult Education Center in California, helping adults pass the General Equivalency Diploma program to obtain the equivalent of a high-school diploma.

Educator Leticia Quezada, born in 1953, is the first Latina elected to serve on the Los Angeles Board of Education. Her campaign centered on support for bilingual education. She was born in Chihuahua, Mexico, her father was a miner and suffered from tuberculosis, dying in 1962 at age 33. Quezada moved to California with her mother and younger sister. Her strong feelings about bilingual programs stem from her own experiences: When she first came to the United States she dropped from a straight A average in Mexico to failing grades in California. "Because of my own experiences as a child who was Spanish-speaking and struggling, poor and powerless, I want to help make a change," she says. Attacked by critics for having interest only in Latino children, she insists, "I think all the children should be bilingual . . . in this . . . multicultural nation."

Most of the very small number of Latino college and university teachers,[16] almost all of them hired since the civil rights struggles of the 1960s, have been pioneers in another important way. In earlier decades, there were no courses on college campuses on the history of Latinos. Students were taught one-sided versions of the history of the West. With the advent of Chicano and Puerto Rican studies departments, the situation began to change. Latino scholars researched and wrote about the lost history of the second-largest minority in the United States.

Since the accomplishments of all women are only fragmentarily recorded, Hispanic women scholars have faced a formidable task of piecing together the history of Latinas. This important work fell on the shoulders of a handful of Latina teacher-scholars like Virginia Sanchez Korrol of Brooklyn College and Altagracia Ortiz of John Jay College,[17] who are concentrating on Puerto Rican women's history; Deena Gonzalez, a leading Chicana historian; Adelaida del Castillo, Margarita B. Melville, and a few others who contribute to the ongoing research on Chicana history.

Many of these educator-activist-scholars did double and triple duty to develop higher education programs for Latinos. A few became administrators of special programs at universities with large Latino student bodies. Isaura Santiago, now president of Hostos Community College (see chapter 5), was born in Brooklyn in 1946. Her parents came to the United States from Puerto Rico, hoping to find better schools for their children. Her mother worked in a factory and encouraged her three daughters to become teachers. Santiago trained as a teacher at Brooklyn College, but when she tried her hand at student teaching, she felt that "Hispanic children were being mistreated." She went to work for ASPIRA, a community-based educational organization organized by Latinas like Antonia Pantoja, the Puerto Rican granddaughter of a tobacco worker. In the late 1960s, Santiago taught elementary education at Hunter College, initiating a graduate bilingual teachers' program. In 1986, she was selected as president of Hostos College, serving the South Bronx.

In the sciences and engineering, traditionally male fields, there are very few Latinos in general and even smaller percentages of Latinas. Ellen Ochoa became the first female Hispanic astronaut in July 1990. Many members of Ochoa's Mexican American family are professionals. "From my mother we were all encouraged to do whatever we wanted to do," Ochoa says. By age 33 she held three patents in optical processing. When NASA graduated the first six women astronauts in 1978, Ochoa applied and was accepted in 1987. She is glad if she inspires other Hispanic youngsters to excel in the sciences.

Margarita H. Colmennares, environmental engineer, was the first woman to become president of the Society of Hispanic Professional Engineers. The eldest of five children of Mexican immigrants from Oaxaca, Mexico, she says, "I have usually been the first woman to hold most of the positions I've had in my career." She works at Chevron, ensuring compliance with government environmental laws. She is eager to see an increase in the number of Latino scientists and engineers, "even if this means reforming the U.S. educational system."

Hispanic magazine, interested in featuring upbeat articles on role models for young Latinos, has devoted considerable space to the accomplishments of Latinas in the business world. The July 1992 "minority business issue" features several "Latinas in Corporate America," some earning six-figure salaries. In other issues, however, a less rosy picture emerges. In an article in October 1992, for example, the author frankly states that of publicly "owned corporate boards . . . only about 41 of 7,199 directors were Hispanic."[18] Most corporate directors are middle-aged white males. In the same issue of the magazine, the column "Focus on Minority Business" quotes a Latina commenting on government loans to minorities: "I thought we could take the SBA and banks seriously, and that there was capital out there to be loaned to us, especially to a Hispanic female. . . . I quickly found out that was not the case. . . . I got a lot of runaround."[19]

Concerning jobs even in the federal government, *Hispanic* published an article in April 1992 complaining that "the National Association of Latino Elected and Appointed Officials reported that Federal employment of Latinos during the 1980s had failed to keep pace with the growth of the Hispanic community . . . professional positions were underrepresented despite the growing number of college-educated Hispanics."[20]

There are some success stories of course, but neither African Americans nor Latinos are well represented in managerial and professional positions—a broadly defined white-collar category. More than 25 percent of all women work in such jobs, but only 15.7 percent of Latinas.

For many Latinos, owning one's own business is a solution to employment problems. Hispanic firms grew in number by 81 percent between 1982 and 1987, but they comprised only about 3 percent of total of 13 million companies. Most of them were small enterprises, earning about 1 percent of the income of all U.S. businesses. Very few were owned by women.[21] Poor youngsters, whether white, black, Asian, or Hispanic, often dream about a glamorous way out of poverty as athletes, entertainers, artists, or writers. Most women know that professional sports—the big-money ones like baseball, football, basketball and boxing—have always been games for men, as both players and owners. Until recently, male tennis players played for money while women played for trophies. Referees and team owners were *always* male. A number of Latinas have helped break the barriers to women in sports. Linda Alvarado, for example, the only daughter in a Mexican American family of six children, born in New Mexico in 1951, is now part owner of the Colorado Rockies. She accumulated the money to buy the baseball team by running a profitable construction firm. "There is a perception that you had to be 6′2″ with muscles like Popeye's to be a contractor. These are myths," she insists.

Puerto Rican Sandra Ortiz-Del Valle is another rarity in the sports world—a referee in professional basketball. At the City University of New York, she played women's basketball and after she graduated, she refereed boys' teams. She now works for the United States Basketball League and hopes to someday referee for the NBA, although she knows that it will be hard to prove herself because she is a woman.

Rosemary Casals, born in 1948 to poor immigrant parents from El Salvador, played a central role in making tennis a paying sport for women. Always uncomfortable with the country-club players dressed in traditional white garb, she donned brightly colored costumes and played competitively, landing invitations to tour professionally. As audiences thronged to watch women tennis players on the courts, Casals and other women tennis players fought and won better fees for female athletes. In the 1990s she was still playing. Teamed with Billie Jean King, she won the U.S. Open Seniors' women's doubles championship. Puerto Rican Gigi Fernandez and Dominican Mary Jo Fernandez are other well-known Latina tennis players.

Since 1978, Mexican American Nancy Lopez has been a professional golfer. She is one of only five women to win more than $1 million in the sport.

Most filmgoers know the names of Latino stars like Lou Diamond Philips and Rosie Perez, but few people are aware of the trailblazers who went before them. From the earliest days of Mexican and Puerto Rican settlements, touring and permanent theater companies have staged Spanish-language productions. Fleeing the violence during the Mexican Revolution, many Mexican theater companies toured Mexican communities in the United States. Los Angeles became a major center for Spanish-language theater in the years before the Great Depression. In Ybor City, Florida, Cuban tobacco workers supported several theater troupes. In the Puerto Rican barrios of the East Coast, theater was also popular. Famous Spanish plays were performed as well as the work of local Latino writers. Vaudeville troupes and circuses also came to Latino neighborhoods, charging reasonable prices and telling their jokes in Spanish.

With the advent of film and the poverty of the Great Depression, Hispanic theater almost disappeared in the 1920s and 1930s. In New York City, it was revived through the efforts of people like Miriam Colón, often called "the first lady of Hispanic theater in New York."

Born in Puerto Rico in 1945, Colón is another of the many Latinas who credits her mother as "the major force in my life." Although she debuted on Broadway in 1953 and soon after landed roles in Hollywood films and television, Colón wanted Spanish-language and bilingual theater available in New York to Latinos who could not afford Broadway's high-priced tickets. She founded the Puerto Rican Traveling Theater and cofounded the Nuevo Círculo Dramático, the first Spanish-language theater in New York. Colon wants to be remembered as someone "who never forgot her people."

No big fortunes are made by Hispanic theater groups.

Most struggle to survive. But without them, Latino playwrights would never see their work produced. Teatro Cuatro, a company of Latinos from several countries of Central America, South America, and the Caribbean, had the good fortune of associating with Joseph Papp's New York Shakespeare Festival. Papp's theater now frequently produces Latino plays. The original troupe also opened its own theater in Spanish Harlem.

Despite these exceptions, there have been very few opportunities for Latino playwrights, actors and directors. In 1965 an extraordinary theater was born when Luis Valdez created El Teatro Campesino, a company of farm workers and students that performed plays dramatizing the grape strike. Many of the amateur actors became professionals, leaving the agricultural fields forever. One-act pieces called *Actos* were almost always on political subjects like bilingual education, racism, or the Vietnam War. Within five years a Chicano theater movement had been born, which holds festivals in the United States and Mexico. With the decline of the Chicano movement, most of the groups had disbanded by the 1980s, but a whole generation of actors, directors and playwrights had been trained and some went on to considerable success.[22]

Two of the best-known Latina playwrights were born in Cuba. María Irene Fornés has won fellowships and Obies for her many plays, ranging from comedies to love stories and musicals. Fornés spends many hours encouraging and teaching young Latino playwrights. Dolores Prida came to the United States as a teenager when her family fled Cuba as opponents of the Cuban Revolution. After fifteen years of working for newspapers and periodicals, Prida came in contact with *Revista Areito,* a publication of young Cubans who wanted improved relations between the United States and Cuba. In 1977, her feminist bilingual musical comedy *Beautiful Señoritas* was produced in New York, its theme the liberation of Latinas from male and Church control. Prida traveled to Cuba in 1978 and

1979 and was part of discussions with Fidel Castro's government that led to visitation rights in Cuba for exiles with relatives there. Prida receives death threats from right-wing Cubans because of her involvement with the project, and her plays are not performed in parts of Florida and New Jersey.

As hundreds of actors headed for Hollywood when they could not find adequate work on the stage, so have many Latinos made the same move. The experiences of Rita Moreno, one of the first Latinas to break into New York theater, are typical of the hardships faced by Latino actors.[23]

Born Rosa Dolores Alverio, in Humacao, Puerto Rico, in 1931, Rita Moreno was brought by her seamstress mother to live in a New York City tenement at the age of five. There she took dancing lessons from Paco Cansino, the uncle of Margarita Carmen Cansino, who later dyed her dark tresses red and became Hollywood "Anglo" glamour queen Rita Hayworth. The talented Alverio girl soon was entertaining in children's theater performances and at weddings. At the age of thirteen, she landed her first small role on Broadway.

Joining the rush to Hollywood, she earned a living dubbing Spanish, and landed a contract with MGM as Rosita Moreno. In dozens of movies in the 1950s she played minor stereotyped roles as Latin "spitfires . . . barefoot with my nostrils flaring," and Indian and Arab maidens, she says in her autobiography. Terribly depressed, she returned to New York. Twentieth Century Fox lured her out to Hollywood once more, only to offer her more of the same. Then, as Rita Moreno, her break came with the part of Puerto Rican Anita in the film version of *West Side Story,* which won her an Oscar for best supporting actress in 1962. But offered no films with Latina characters after that success, she left to act on the London stage. When she returned, the civil rights activities of Latino actors gave her more opportunities in films and television. Often she crossed over into "Anglo" parts, but says, "never, not for one minute, have I forgotten where I came from or who I am. . . . When I was a young starlet, I wanted to be an all-American girl. . . . But when I grew up and developed a sense of self-esteem as a Hispanic, I learned how essential it was to cling to one's own heritage, for only in that way can we . . . ultimately understand ourselves."

Before the late 1960s, Latino performers all faced similar problems. Male actors could play bit parts as lazy Mexicans, villainous criminals, fools, or skirt-chasing "gay caballeros." Mexican actress Lupe Vélez became the official "Mexican Spitfire." Lighter-skinned actresses like Rita Hayworth and Raquel Welch changed their names and "passed."

During the post–World War II cold war period, except for a few independent films like *Salt of the Earth* (1954), depicting a 1951–1952 New Mexico mine strike, films about social problems were not produced.

Latino civil rights activists successfully protested against stereotypes like Frito Bandito and Chiquita Banana in television commercials. Latinos were only three percent of the work force in Hollywood, a lowly three percent in radio and television broadcasting.[24]

In the 1970s, a Chicano documentary cinema emerged. Occasionally the name of a Latina would appear in the credits. There were a few exceptions, such as Sylvia Morales, whose 1979 film *Chicana* traces the history of Mexicanas and Chicanas. Her documentary on AIDS, *SIDA,* has been shown on public television. Elvia M. Alvarado's *Una mujer* was enthusiastically received at the Chicano Film Festival in 1984.

In the growing Puerto Rican film industry, women are becoming better known. Ana María García directed *La operación* (The Operation, 1982) on the sterilization of Puerto Rican women.

Although the best-known Latino performers are men

like Raul Julia and Ruben Blades, in recent years, there have been some success stories about Latina performers. Priscilla Lopez is best known for her portrayal of Diane Morales in *Chorus Line.*

Rosie Perez, one of ten children from a musical Puerto Rican Brooklyn family, attended college in Los Angeles and majored in biochemistry. She was spotted dancing at a Latin club, and was invited to appear on *Soul Train.* Her innovative dancing brought her choreographing assignments, including one at a posh dance club. Filmmaker Spike Lee noticed her and asked her to play opposite him as Tina in *Do the Right Thing.* In *White Men Can't Jump* her role was originally written for an Anglo. "Minorities can play regular roles too," Perez says. "And being a minority you have a responsibility to help other minorities along the way."

Once a few films on Hispanic themes like *La Bamba* or the serious *Stand and Deliver* and *The Milagro Beanfield War,* succeeded at the box office, "Hispanic Hollywood" emerged. Along with Latino actors like Emilio Estevez, some new Latina stars appeared, including Maria Conchita Alonso, Rachel Ticotin, and Rosana de Soto.

In 1992, sixty-year-old Chita Rivera starred in Broadway's musical version of *Kiss of the Spider Woman,* a play about revolution in Latin America. Born in Puerto Rico in 1933, Rivera first gained fame playing the stage role of Anita in *West Side Story* in 1957. In the mid-1980s, she won a Tony Award.

Latina newscasters are now appearing on national networks. One of the best known is Giselle Fernandez, who became a correspondent on the "CBS Evening News" in 1992. Born in 1961 in Mexico City, she came to East Los Angeles with her family when she was four. Working her way up from internships on radio stations, Fernandez came to national attention as one of the anchors of "CBS This Morning."

Called "a new voice in mainstream American literature," Chicana Sandra Cisneros was raised in Chicago. "If I had lived up to my teachers' expectations," she says, "I'd still be working in a factory." She wrote in secret. In her collection of short fiction, *Woman Hollering Creek and Other Stories* (1991), she says she tried to include "as many different kinds of Latinos as possible so that mainstream America could see how diverse we are."

Judith Ortiz Cofer, whose poem appears in chapter 4, was determined to write poetry in English despite the fact that she learned it as her second language. Her first novel, *The Line of the Sun,* tells the story of three generations of a Puerto Rican family and was highly praised for its poetic quality.

Nicholasa Mohr has achieved prominence in the field of children's literature, winning countless awards for such touching books as *Nilda,* the story of a poor Puerto Rican young girl living in New York's El Barrio during World War II. Mohr began as a free-lance artist for book publishers. In 1975, she published *El Bronx Remembered,* treating subjects that are usually avoided, such as interracial relations, homosexuality, and racism.

There are many talented Latino artists. But to succeed in the world of art it is necessary to have connections with art galleries and museums. Lacking these, Latinos developed their own networks and their own specialty, mural painting, during the 1960s and early 1970s. Inspired by the example of famous Mexican muralists like Diego Rivera,[25] Latinos created highly original murals on walls and buildings, where they could be seen by everyone. Major museums began to pay attention to these talented artists, and some of their smaller works were exhibited.

Judith F. Baca is famous for her huge murals, the "Great Wall" and "World Wall." A second-generation Chicana born in Los Angeles in 1946, she was raised by her mother and grandmother. She became a teacher in the Catholic parochial school she had attended as a child, and she joined the movement against the Vietnam War. Fired for her antiwar activism, Baca eventually found a job with the City of Los Angeles Cultural Affairs Division. With about twenty young people, many of them gang members, she painted murals. At the Social and Public Art Resource Center (SPARC) in Venice, California, that she helped to found, many young people have been trained to paint.

Patricia Rodriguez is another successful Chicana artist who makes major efforts to help young Latinos. Her parents were migrant workers, and she did not attend school full time until she was 13, still illiterate. Again, one teacher made the difference by pushing her to pursue art. After earning her teaching credentials, she developed the first course in Chicano art history at the University of California. Rodriguez's work is displayed in the permanent collections of several museums. Her personal success is not enough for her. Rodriguez is upset that others are not included: "We pay for these public institutions with our tax dollars; therefore, we should have equal voice and opportunities."

Latinismo, the cultural blending together of several Hispanic groups, is most pronounced in the world of music. While Latinos were being barred from jobs and equal housing and stereotyped in Hollywood, people everywhere were dancing to the rhythms of Latin America—from the Argentine tango to the Caribbean salsa—and buying recordings made by Latino musicians.

Jazz was created by African American, African Cuban, and Latino jazz musicians. Alcide "Yellow" Nuñez, jazz clarinetist, launched Dixieland jazz with his Dixieland Jazz Band. The big band sound of Tommy Dorsey, Artie Shaw, Duke Ellington, and dozens of others in the late 1930s adopted the Cuban folk form known as the *son.* The contagious Caribbean rhythms are part of the Latino jazz/rock movement of musicians like Chick Corea and Carlos Santana.

Salsa (sauce) refers to the "hot" rhythms of Afro-Caribbean music in general. It contains elements of jazz and African religious music as well as elements of the big band sound. Origins of salsa can be found in a wide range of Latino music, from the songs of Puerto Rican sugarcane workers to Tito Rodriguez's recordings of the late 1950s.

Celia Cruz, called the "undisputed queen of salsa," has been performing for forty years. After winning a talent show in the late 1940s in Cuba, she went on to fame as a nightclub headliner there. She left Cuba after the 1959 revolution, entertaining first in Mexico and then the United States. Most young Latinos were more interested in rock and roll than in Cruz's Latin music, and she was unknown until Tito Puente, the "King of Latin Swing," helped her after he heard her powerful voice on the radio. In the early 1970s, when salsa became popular, so did Cruz, who was named best female vocalist by *Billboard* in 1978. She has continued her career, inspiring singing stars like Gloria Estefan.

Composers of popular music and show tunes like Irving Berlin, Cole Porter, and Jerome Kern are known by millions, but there is a Latina songwriter who also wrote hundreds of well-known songs. Maria Grever (1894–1951), born in Mexico City, composed dozens of film scores and lyrics for Broadway shows. People who hum songs like "Volvere," "What a Difference a Day Makes," and "Magic Is the Moonlight," rarely know that a Mexican woman created them.

There are many other Latina hit singers and songwriters. Linda Ronstadt has sung and recorded a wide variety of music—pop, rock, folk, opera, operetta, and Mariachi. Born in Tucson, Arizona, in 1946, she decided to be a singer when she was six, singing along with her father when he played recordings of Mexican singers. She says that her Spanish is not very good because "When we were little, we spoke Spanish at home, but the schools pounded it out of us pretty early." Nevertheless, she recorded an album of her father's favorite songs in Spanish in 1987, *Canciones de mi padre*. Mexican American Grammy winner Vikki Carr, who joined Ronstadt to perform with Mariachi groups, is another singer whose popularity has endured.

There are many recent Latina music stars. Maria Conchita Alonso, born in Cuba in 1957 but raised in Venezuela, has won Grammy nominations and has a gold album. Singer and dancer Martika (Marta Marrero), is the daughter of Cuban immigrants.

Sheila Escovedo, who goes by the stage name of Sheila E., is called by *Ebony* "probably the hottest female drummer in the business." Two of her albums have gone gold. Her father is Pete Escovedo, famous drummer with the rock group Santana. Sheila E. concentrates on Latin jazz.[26]

Two Cuban-born ballet dancers reflect the continuing tension over the Cuban Revolution. Alicia Alonso, born in the early 1920s, studied in New York City at the School of American Ballet and with several famous ballet dancer-teachers. In the late 1930s she appeared in Broadway musicals and gained fame as a dancer with the American Ballet Company. In 1948 she returned to Cuba and founded her own ballet company, a showcase for Cuban talent. When dictator Fulgencio Batista cut the company's subsidy, they were forced to disband. She went on international tour, returning to her country after the Cuban Revolution in 1959 just as most wealthy and middle-class Cubans were leaving. The new regime encouraged her training of young people, and Alonso was happy: "A rural child [in Cuba] has an equal opportunity with a city child. If there is dance talent, we will find it." In 1990, at the approximate age of seventy, she performed in *Swan Lake* at the American Ballet Theater's 50th anniversary gala, to rave reviews.

Lourdes Lopez, born in Cuba in 1958, is now a principal dancer for the New York City Ballet Company. Her father was a soldier in dictator Batista's army who fled with his family in 1959.

Dancer and choreographer Tina Ramirez, of Mexican-Puerto Rican heritage, mixes Latino versions of modern dance and ballet in the performances of the group she founded in 1970, New York's Ballet Hispánico. "Why not draw from twenty-one nations instead of two?" she says. The group has trained hundreds of students.

Millions went to see the movie version of Bizet's opera *Carmen* in 1984.[27] The title role was played by Julia Migenes-Johnson, a young opera singer from New York City's Spanish Harlem, opposite the better-known Mexican opera star Placido Domingo. In a true live Cinderella story, Migenes-Johnson worked her way up right to the stage of the prestigious Metropolitan Opera.

The vast majority of talented musicians remains unrecognized. When the San Diego-based Border Arts Workshop *"Cafe Urgente"* performed in Buffalo, New York, in 1991, the audience was swept away by the stirring Latino songs of a farm worker who spontaneously contributed to a jam session at the end of the evening. She was introduced as "Lares," and told a few people later that she is a homeless Puerto Rican more than sixty years of age who was in the area picking tomatoes. She had never performed on a real stage before, singing only for her homeless friends in the New York City subways or for farm workers in the fields. She was involved in an area movement to name a street after a migrant woman worker as a sign of respect for the area's farm workers.[28]

Lares is more representative of Latinas than the professionals and artists described above are. The vast majority of Latinas are poor. Probably the most prosperous group taken as a whole are the estimated one million Cubans now living in the United States. There are several reasons for this. For one thing, when the Cuban Revolution ended the Batista dictatorship in 1959, many of those who fled to the United States were middle or upper class, better educated than Puerto Ricans and Mexicans, and with much more money to invest.

Even more significant is the fact that U.S. immigration policy follows State Department foreign policy very closely. Lower-class (and darker-complexioned) Haitians or Central Americans were turned away, as were Chileans and Dominicans opposing U.S.-supported dictatorships.[29] The barriers to immigration were not only lifted for anti-Castro Cubans, but many unexpected prizes awaited new arrivals: relocation payments for those who wanted to settle outside of Miami; scholarships and business loans; special job training and English-language instruction. In Chicago, Cuban teachers were assisted in finding teaching jobs and Cuban workers were hired to break a strike at Motorola.[30]

Many non-Cuban Latinos, as well as Miami's economically disadvantaged African Americans, resented the special treatment accorded the Cubans. This was one of the causes of riots in the black ghetto of Miami in the 1980s.

More than 100,000 darker-skinned and poorer Cubans arrived in the United States in 1980. Called "Marielitos" (sailing from the port of Mariel), they were eligible for entry and aid under the new Refugee Assistance Act of 1980, which defined them as "political refugees." Among the new arrivals, mostly working people, were some criminals released from Cuba's jails, which displeased both the State Department and the better-off Cubans in Miami.

Even in the mainly anti-Castro Cuban community in Miami, there were Cubans who disagreed with U.S. policy. Writer Lourdes Casal, who died of kidney disease in 1981 at the age of 43, organized the Antonio Maceo Brigade, a group of young Cuban exiles who wanted to establish ties with Cuba. In 1978 Casal helped convince the Cuban government to allow exiles to visit their families in Cuba.

In Cuba, Casal had joined the student movement (26th of July Movement) to help overthrow Batista. She came to the United States in 1961 because she opposed the socialist programs of the Castro regime after the victorious revolution in 1959. She changed her mind about the Castro regime during her research work for the magazine *Revista Areito* when she made two trips to Cuba and saw the many gains achieved in education, housing, and free health care.

Unlike the Cubans, most refugees from Central America and Latin America were not welcomed. Those few who were permitted to stay enjoyed no special privileges. The only exceptions were the Nicaraguans who had opposed the 1979 Nicaraguan Revolution. Most of the others, denied political refugee status, remained among the "have-nots"—society's growing bottom tier of poor people.

A number of Salvadorans, Guatemalans, and Haitians were herded into detention camps described by human rights groups as "concentration camps."[31] Yet many were fleeing for their lives from U.S.-backed military dictatorships. Death squads throughout Latin America were killing tens of thousands of innocent people suspected of being "pro-Communist."[32] The U.S. government usually supported Latin America's dictatorships as a "lesser evil," the alternative to revolution. More than 100,000 Americans, including several Latinas, formed the Sanctuary Movement in the 1980s to provide "safe houses" for the Central Americans. By 1991, the movement won a government concession of temporary political refugee status for most Salvadorans.

Today, there are probably about 2 million recently arrived Central Americans living in different parts of the United States. Together with South Americans, they make up 13.7 percent of the nation's Latino population.

Large numbers work as maids, gardeners, seamstresses, and low-wage service or industrial employees. Others are professionals.

Also crowding the ranks of the "have-nots" are Dominicans—an estimated one million. Most Dominicans are in the U.S. legally, but others came on student or tourist visas and stayed. They are always subject to deportation. Some fled the government imposed by U.S. troops in 1965, but most came to escape the subsequent increase in poverty on their beautiful Caribbean island. Many reside in New York City's Washington Heights barrio, located near the George Washington Bridge. In many ways it resembles the old *colonias* of the Puerto Ricans, with its own shops, restaurants, and other businesses, usually run by successful Dominican men, with many women taking in boarders and piecework. The media has emphasized the drug dealers. Most Dominicans, however, work long hours to send money home and hate the drug traffic that plagues their neighborhoods.

Three-fifths of the recently arrived Dominicans are women, often very young. They earn only a third of the salaries paid to white women. They take jobs as maids or in non-union factories and unsafe garment sweatshops. Their incomes average around $8,000 a year, a few thousand less than the Dominican male averages.[33]

Of all the different Latino groups among the "have-nots," farm workers remain the worst off. Over the years, the UFW, like other unions, lost several thousand members during a prolonged antiunion offensive by employers. Nationally, membership in labor unions plummeted from over 30 percent of the work force in the 1960s to about 15 percent in the 1990s.

Dolores Huerta married Richard Chavez, Cesar Chavez's brother, during the grape boycott and gave birth to four more children while continuing her nonstop activities, lobbying the California state government for enforcement of the new farm labor law. To extend the

UFW's educational campaigns, Huerta was instrumental in founding Radio Campesina, KUFW, the union's radio station.

The pesticide issue became the central focus of Huerta's work. Low-flying airplanes dust crops with dangerous pesticides that are blown by the wind for miles. Earlier, the farm workers had won a ban against DDT and a few other deadly pesticides, lending momentum to a mushrooming environmentalist movement. But as new generations of farm workers' children were born with birth defects from the remaining legal pesticides, the UFW had to call for another grape boycott in 1986. With short videos like "Wrath of Grapes,"[34] it educated the public to the dangers of eating captan-sprayed fruit. UFW publications like *Food and Justice* explained how most birth defects are genetically caused during the early months of pregnancy—often when a farm worker may not even know she is pregnant. Images of legless children, crying mothers, and cancer deaths of teenagers in towns near the sprayed farm fields dramatized the awful reality. Yet a conservative governor in California refused to sign a bill that would have required growers to post signs warning about pesticides.

Worse yet, in 1988 Dolores Huerta and other peaceful demonstrators were clubbed by police in San Francisco as presidential candidate George Bush campaigned there. Huerta was severely beaten and hospitalized after emergency surgery. She resumed activity in the 1990s, helping to win a ban on a few of the more offensive pesticides.[35]

Meanwhile, to try to escape the jurisdiction of the strongest unions and increase their profit rates, employers were transfering nearly two thousand assembly plants to Mexico and importing low-wage Mexican and Caribbean immigrant workers for the nation's farms, services, and select areas of the remaining factories (often subcontracted workshops).[36] A number of Latino labor organizers, including former UFW leaders, responded by trying to organize the "undocumented" immigrant workers. They formed an independent cluster of new unions called the American Federation of Workers (AFW). Active in several states, the AFW grew to more than forty thousand members, many of them Latinas.[37]

The "new unionism", as it was called, began developing in many parts of the country. Latinas were very active in it. As early as 1974 some four thousand Latinas in Texas won a lengthy strike for union representation against the huge blue-jeans manufacturer, Farah Clothing Company. In Arizona, the Morenci Miners Women's Auxiliary, led by Mexican Americans like Fina Roman, stood up to Phelps Dodge when it tried to break the area's thirteen unions. On a national speaking tour, Roman explained to packed auditoriums: "It is 'we the people'—the old, the poor, the average—who have become scapegoats for the greed of the industrial giants."[38]

The mine women's peaceful picket lines and noisy protests infuriated Phelps Dodge bosses. An Arizona policeman fumed: "If we could just get rid of those broads, we'd have it made."[39] The women were frequently arrested at unexpected times and thrown in jail. Diane Delgado said the hard part was explaining it to the children: "I told them I was doing this so they wouldn't have to go through it all again when they were older."[40] Rather than give in, Phelps Dodge cut back its production. The women and the striking miners later won several suits against the company for violations of their constitutional rights.

In 1991, Latinas and others struck the giant nut company, Diamond Walnut, in Texas. Diamond dismissed the strikers and replaced them permanently. The women became leading spokespeople for a new law that would ban the permanent replacement of striking workers. No more unfair "One strike and you're out!" they argued. Until such a new law was passed, the laid-off strikers were asking the public to boycott Diamond products.

María Elena Durazo became the first woman, Latina or Anglo, to become president of a major union in Los Angeles when she was elected as president of the majority Latino membership Hotel and Restaurant Employees Local 11. Born around 1954, she traveled and picked crops with her parents, both migrant farm workers, suffering cold, malnourishment, and all the other hardships of farm workers' children. Involved in the Chicano movement, she heard about the Los Angeles People's College of Law, dedicated to providing education to the children of poor whites, blacks, and Latinos, and she earned a law degree from there in the 1970s. After becoming an organizer and arbitrator for Local ll, she discovered that its leaders refused to hold bilingual meetings and were not popular with the Latina workers. After ten years of internal struggle to change and save the union, Durazo was elected a president in 1989. One Latina in the union said of her, "María Elena has made us realize that united we can take control and run things the way we want."

The low wages of Latinas have led them to union organizing in the middle of a general decline in unionization in the United States. Today, there are about 1.3 million Latinos in labor unions, roughly the same number as whites. Latina women outnumber white women by two to one.[41] The AFL-CIO says Latinas are entering the labor force at twice the rate of all U.S. women. If the declining labor movement is ever fully reinvigorated, it will probably be because of the ongoing courageous struggles of the Latinas.

In New York City, Latina and African American women employed not only in hospitals but in other patient-care facilities joined the nation's largest independent union: District 1199 of the national Drug, Hospital and Health Care Employees Union. Led by Puerto Rican Dennis Rivera, the 100,000-member District 1199 is now a strong voice for health care reform and workers' rights.[42]

Most of the health workers are especially concerned about the health status of Latinas.

In 1983, a new organization formed solely around the issue of Latinas' health. Mexican American Luz Alvarez Martinez became the director of the Organización Nacional de La Salud de La Mujer Latina (National Latina Health Organization). Alvarez Martinez was busy raising a family during the 1960s and did not get involved in the Chicano movement. In 1977, with her children older, she returned to school and became involved with the Berkeley Women's Health Collective, a feminist clinic.

In 1983, suffering from health problems, she went to the hospital for a tubal ligation. An English-language film informed women that there were contraceptive methods available if they wished to avoid sterilization. The Spanish-language version emphasized sterilization. Angry at this outrageous difference, in 1986 Alvarez Martinez and three other Latinas decided to apply for a grant and create a bilingual health information service. Alvarez Martinez went on to create a center for battered Latinas, since few existing centers offered services in Spanish.

The economic downturns of the early 1990s have provoked new tides of anti-immigrant feeling. As desperate people look for scapegoats, farm workers and many immigrant members of the new unions become targets. In 1986, Congress passed the Immigration Reform and Control Law (IRCA).[43] The employer sanctions clause banned the hiring of "undocumented" workers, whose labor rights in the past had been recognized by several court decisions. IRCA's fine print, on the other hand, allowed the legal importation of farm workers and others when needed—a form of contract labor outlawed a hundred years earlier.

An antidiscrimination clause in IRCA failed to stem anti-Latino racism. Some employers openly acknowledged that they turned away citizens because of their

Spanish surnames rather than risk sanctions. Unemployment among Latinos rose in 1987 even faster than among blacks.

IRCA's amnesty clause offered a lengthy step-by-step legalization process for those immigrants able to prove continuous residence in the U.S. since 1982. Because most had been hiding from the Immigration and Naturalization Services, it was not easy for them to make a strong amnesty case. Women found it especially difficult, since often they had come later than 1982, *after* their male relatives. Many faced immediate deportation without their husbands or their new citizen children born in the United States after their arrival. Because so many Latinos complained about their families being broken up, the INS later moved the year for proof of residence up to 1988. That still left millions of "illegal" women working in sweatshops with the difficult problem of proving their presence here. Their employers were not willing to vouch for their work because the sweatshops were in violation of so many labor laws.

Employers also used IRCA to break up the new unions of "undocumented" workers. Employees expressing pro-union sentiments were fired or threatened with deportation.[44] The end result of IRCA was to drive millions of "illegals" further underground without even the protections of labor laws that they had been granted in the pre-IRCA days. Cases of outright slavery were reported as early as 1990.[45] Anti-immigrant "hate crimes" spread. Local television stations reported on Ku Klux Klan attacks against immigrants crossing the Mexican border; San Diego teenagers shooting at Mexicans "for sport"; Border Patrol agents murdering or wounding fleeing immigrants. In a report entitled "Frontier Justice," Americas Watch, a prominent human rights group, denounced the Justice Department for its failure to adequately monitor human rights complaints.[46]

Poverty among Latinos worsened in the 1980s and

1990s. Latinos taken as a whole are near the bottom of the nation's economic pyramid, their unemployment rate only slightly below that of African Americans. A few figures give the picture for poverty in general and Latinos in particular:

- 1980–1987: The income of the poorest 20 percent of the nation plummeted by 10 percent, while that of the wealthiest 20 percent rose by 16 percent;
- Today, 14.5 percent of Americans live in poverty and more than 20 million go hungry;
- One million of the nation's children are homeless; twelve million children suffer hunger;
- *38.4 percent of Latino children and nearly half of black children live in poverty;*
- Puerto Ricans' poverty level surpasses 40 percent, compared with blacks' 32 percent, all Latinos' 28 percent, and whites' 10.7 percent. 56.7 percent of Puerto Rican children are poor.[47]

One-sixth of all families in the United States are female-headed—for Mexicans and Mexican Americans the figure is one-fifth, and for Puerto Ricans two-fifths. The prolonged economic crisis of the 1980s and 1990s has especially impacted on women, since they earn less than 58 percent of what men earn for equivalent work. Minority women are hit even harder. As the garment industry and other jobs that minority women have traditionally held move overseas, they are forced to take even lower paying jobs or join the swelling ranks of the unemployed. Among "the working poor"—those employed but at wages leaving them below the poverty line—women vastly outnumber men.

Unemployment has hit young people especially hard. Because of it, youth gangs have changed completely in the past twenty years. With entry-level jobs in unionized industries no longer available, young gang members continue to stay on the streets into their twenties, thirties, and even middle years. Many unemployed youths turn to drug dealing and other criminal activities, counting on their gang members back home when they are sent off to jail. Young women, who in earlier decades were briefly the girlfriends of gang members and then married and escaped from street life, are today in gangs of their own in many cities. Most are high school dropouts. The gangs substitute for families, unavailable jobs, and lost dreams of the future.[48]

The economic gap between a few well-off, usually white or light-skinned, Latinos and poor Latinos has continued to widen (even as the gap between rich and poor has done among all groups, including whites).[49] A "white backlash" has gained momentum. In the 1980s and 1990s, court decisions by conservative appointees of Reagan and Bush reflected the backlash and rolled back many of the gains of the civil rights movement.[50]

Much of the mass media once called the 1980s "the decade of the Hispanic." Antonia Hernández of MALDEF recently countered: "The 1980s was not the decade of the Hispanic. . . . We need to move. Otherwise we'll develop into a community with a small middle class and a large poverty class."

Many believe that sad state of affairs already exists. They hope that, before it is too late, a new and better movement will develop to turn things around to make the United States a better place for *everyone*. Latinas, among the most deprived of the "American Dream," will surely be prominent in the ranks of such a movement.

Source Notes

Introduction

1. Introduction of the word "Hispanic" was an attempt to depoliticize Latino activists in the civil rights movement of the 1960s and 1970s who had introduced rebellious names like "Chicano" and "Boriqua" for Mexican Americans and Puerto Ricans. "Chicano" was the word traditionally used by the working class to refer to itself and by richer Mexican Americans to put down the lower class—*see* Rodolfo Acuña, *Occupied America: A History of Chicanos* (New York: HarperCollins Publishers, third ed., 1988), ix. "Boricua" means Puerto Rican and derives from the ancient Indian name for the island of Puerto Rico. For more details on the diversity of Latinos, *see* Joan Moore and Harry Pachon, *Hispanics in the United States* (Englewood Cliffs: Prentice-Hall, Inc., 1985), p. 3, and Rubén G. Rumbaut, "The Americans: Latin American and Caribbean Peoples in the United States," *in* Alfred Stepan, ed., *Americas* (New York: Oxford University Press, 1992), tables on pp. 287 and 288.

2. Recognizing that most other Americans perceive them as one lumped together group, many Spanish-speaking people in the United States use their preferred self-descriptions when they are talking to American and Spanish-speaking friends—Nicaraguan, Chilean, Puerto

Rican, or whatever—and the "official" Hispanic or Latino title with others. In this book, we will do likewise, preferring "Latino" to the politically tinged and misleading "Hispanic."

3. Quoted in Mary G. Harris, *Cholas: Latino Girls and Gangs* (New York: AMS Press, 1988), p. 58.

4. Alfredo Mirandé and Evangelina Enríquez, *La Chicana: The Mexican-American Woman* (Chicago: University of Chicago Press, 1979), pp. 108–117. Traditionally, fathers in Spain, Italy and other Catholic countries would not allow their daughters to see young men without the presence of a chaperon. When they immigrated to the United States, they continued to maintain the same watchful eye. In Protestant countries like Sweden, men were the legal guardians of their child wives. Hendrick Ibsen wrote his famous play *A Doll's House* about just such a relationship and the wife's vengeance.

For more on the stereotyping of Latinos and Latinas, see Edna Acosta-Belén, *The Puerto Rican Woman* (New York: Praeger Publishers, 1979), pp. 124-125; Francesco Cordasco and Eugene Bucchioni, eds. *The Puerto Rican Experience* (Totowa: Rowman and Littlefield, 1973), pp. 67-71, 80.

5. Adelaida del Castillo, ed., *Between Borders: Essays on Mexicana/Chicana History* (Encino: Floricanto Press, 1990), pp. 459, 464. For more on Flores Magón and the PLM, see James D. Cockcroft, *Intellectual Precursors of the Mexican Revolution* (Austin: University of Texas Press, 1966).

6. *Hispanic,* March 1993, p. 14.

One

1. Quoted in David Montejano, *Anglos and Mexicans in the Making of Texas, 1836–1986* (Austin: University of Texas Press, 1987), p. 14.

2. Quoted in Montejano, p. 27.

3. For more details of this period, *see* Gilberto

López y Rivas, *The Chicanos* (New York: Monthly Review Press, 1973), pp. 27–29.

4. Quoted in Douglas Monroy, "They Didn't Call them 'Padre' for Nothing: Patriarchy in Hispanic California," *in* Adelaida del Castillo, ed., *Between Borders: Essays on Mexicana/Chicana History* (Encino: Floricanto Press, 1990), p. 435.

5. For more details, *see* Helen Lara-Cea, "Notes on the Use of Parish Registers in the Reconstruction of Chicana History in California Prior to 1850, *in* Adelaida del Castillo, ed., *Between Borders: Essays on Mexicana/Chicana History* (Encino: Floricanto Press, 1990), pp. 131–159.

6. This story is a retelling of Ramón A. Gutiérrez, "Marriage and Seduction in Colonial New Mexico," *in* del Castillo, pp. 447–455.

7. Quoted in Gutiérrez, *in* del Castillo, p. 452.

8. Quoted in Gutiérrez, *in* del Castillo, p. 454–455.

9. Rodolfo Acuña, *Occupied America: A History of Chicanos* (New York: HarperCollins Publishers, 1988), p. 55; Rosaura Sánchez and Rosa Martinez Cruz, *Essays on La Mujer* (Los Angeles: University of California Chicano Studies Center Publications, 1977), pp. 100–105.

10. Quoted in Gilberto López y Rivas, *The Chicanos* (New York: Monthly Review Press, 1973), p. 17.

11. James D. Cockcroft, *Mexico* (New York; Monthly Review Press, 1990), p. 71; Howard Zinn, *A People's History of the United States* (New York: Harper-Collins Publishers, 1990), p. 151.

12. Quoted in Acuña, p. 16.

13. Quoted in Acuña, p. 13.

14. Quoted in Carey McWilliams, *North from Mexico* (New York: Greenwood Press, Publishers, 1968), p. 102.

15. For more details on the Mexican American War, *see* Cockcroft, pp. 72–73 and Zinn, pp. 147–156.

16. For more details, *see* Sánchez and Cruz, pp. 100–105.

17. Antonia I. Castañeda, "The Political Economy

of Nineteenth Century Stereotypes of Californians," *in* Del Castillo, pp. 226–227.

18. *See* Acuña, pp. 118–119.

19. Quoted in Acuña, p. 39.

20. Quoted in Acuña, p. 59.

21. For more details of the struggle for justice in the Southwest, *see* James D. Cockcroft, *Hispanics in the Struggle for Social Justice* (New York: Franklin Watts, 1994).

22. Quoted in Del Castillo, p. 135. *See also* pp. 222–223.

23. Quoted in Joan Moore and Harry Panchon, *Hispanics in the United States* (Englewood Cliffs, New Jersey: Prentice-Hall, Inc., 1985), p. 5.

24. For more details, see Del Castillo, pp. 440–441.

25. Quoted in Diana Telgen and Jim Kamp, eds., *Notable Hispanic American Women* (Detroit: Gale Research Inc., 1993), p. 308.

26. For details see Acuña, p. 89.

Two

1. The historical facts in this chapter are based on Rodolfo Acuña, *Occupied America: A History of Chicanos* (New York: HarperCollins Publishers, 1988); James D. Cockcroft, *Hispanics in the Struggle for Social Justice* (New York: Franklin Watts, 1994) ; Alfredo Mirandé and Evangelina Enríquez, *La Chicana: The Mexican-American Woman* (Chicago: University of Chicago Press, 1979); Howard Zinn, *A People's History of the United States* (New York: HarperPerennial, 1990), pp. 247–289.

2. Quoted in Richard O. Boyer and Herbert M. Morais, *Labor's Untold Story* (New York: United Electrical, Radio & Machine Workers of America, 1955), p. 102.

3. Quoted in Boyer and Morais, p. 101.

4. For more on Lucy Parsons, *see* Mirandé and Enríquez, pp. 86–95; Carolyn Ashbaugh, *Lucy Parsons,*

American Revolutionary (Chicago: Charles H. Kerr Publishing Co, 1976).

5. For the full story on Mexican workers, see books by Acuña and Cockcroft in footnote 1; also, James D. Cockcroft, *Outlaws in the Promised Land: Mexican Immigrant Workers and America's Future* (New York: Grove, 1988).

6. For further details on the life of Teresa Urrea, *see* Mirandé and Enríquez, p. 86; Diane Telgen and Jim Kamp, eds., *Hispanic American Women* (Detroit: Gale Research Inc., 1993), pp. 405–406.

7. On the IWW, see Dan Georgakas, *Solidarity Forever: The IWW Reconsidered* (Chicago: Lakeview Press, 1985).

8. James D. Cockcroft, *Intellectual Precursors of the Mexican Revolution* (Austin: University of Texas Press, 1968), p. 134. Cockcroft's book is a pioneering work on the history of the PLM.

9. Quoted in Margarita B. Melville, ed., *Twice a Minority: Mexican American Women* (St. Louis: C.V. Mosby, Inc., 1980), p. 223.

10. For details on these PLM women, *see* Mirandé and Enríquez, pp. 204–205.

11. For more on Ramirez, *see* Mirandé and Enríquez, pp. 206–207; Telgen and Kamp, pp. 330–331.

12. Emma M. Pérez, " 'A La Mujer': A Critique of the Partido Liberal Mexicano's Gender Ideology on Women," *in* Adelaida del Castillo, ed., *Between Borders: Essays on Mexicana/Chicana History* (Encino: Floricanto Press, 1990), p. 473.

13. For additional comments on this belief, *see* Mirandé and Enríquez, pp. 215–216.

14. *See also* Nicolás Kanellos, ed., *The Hispanic-American Almanac* (Detroit: Gale Research Inc., 1993), p. 308.

15. For more details about this period, *see* Bettina

Aptheker, *Woman's Legacy* (Amherst: University of Massachusetts Press, 1982), pp. 64–66; and Melville, pp. 218–224.

16. Quoted in Pérez, *in* Del Castillo, p. 468.

17. Quoted in Acuña, p. 153.

18. For more on the "revolving door," see Cockcroft, *Outlaws*, pp. 15–16, 42–93.

19. Quoted in Acuña, p. 163.

20. For more on this, *see* Kanellos, p. 36. On the Puerto Ricans drafted to fight World War I, see chapter 4.

21. Quoted in Acuña, p. 168.

22. Quoted in Acuña, p. 157.

23. For more on LULAC, *see* Cockcroft, *Hispanics in the Struggle;* and Benjamin Márquez, *LULAC* (Austin: University of Texas Press, 1993).

Three

1. Quoted in Howard Zinn, *A People's History of the United States* (New York: HarperPerennial, 1990), pp. 390–391. For more on the 1930s' Great Depression, *see* Zinn, pp. 378–382.

2. For the history of the eugenics movement, *see* Gena Corea. *The Hidden Malpractice* (New York: Harper & Row, 1977), pp. 126–133. On its use against Latinos, see James D. Cockcroft, *Hispanics in the Struggle for Social Justice* (New York: Franklin Watts, 1994).

3. Quoted in Rodolfo Acuña, *Occupied America: A History of Chicanos* (New York: HarperCollins Publishers, 1988), p. 201.

4. Quoted in Acuña, p. 164.

5. For full coverage of Mexican immigrant workers in the United States, *see* James D. Cockcroft, *Outlaws in the Promised Land: Mexican Immigrant Workers and America's Future* (New York: Grove, 1988).

6. *See* Acuña, pp. 213–215.

7. Quoted in Devra Anne Weber, "Mexican Women on Strike: Memory, History and Oral Narratives"

in Adelaida del Castillo, ed., *Between Borders: Essays on Mexicana/Chicana History* (Encino: Floricanto Press, 1990), p. 183.

8. For more details, *see* Acuña, pp. 210–220; and Cockcroft, *Hispanics.*

9. For details, *see* Acuña, 229.

10. Alfredo Mirandé and Evangelina Enríquez, *La Chicana: The Mexican-American Woman* (Chicago: University of Chicago Press, 1979), p. 118.

11. Louise Año Nuevo Kerr, "Chicanas in the Great Depression," *in* del Castillo, pp. 257–268.

12. Acuña, pp. 225–227; and Diana Telgen and Jim Kamp, eds., *Notable Hispanic American Women* (Detroit: Gale Research Inc., 1993), pp. 398–399.

13. For more, *see* Vicki L. Ruiz, "A Promise Fulfilled: Mexican Cannery Workers in Southern California," *in* del Castillo, pp. 281–298.

14. Author's personal experience.

15. For more on Fierro de Bright, other Latinas, and El Congreso, *see* Mario T. García, *Mexican Americans: Leadership, Ideology, and Identity, 1930–1960* (New Haven: Yale University Press, 1989), pp. 145–174.

16. Quoted in García, p. 153.

17. Nicolás Kanellos, ed., *The Hispanic-American Almanac* (Detroit: Gale Research Inc., 1993), p. 330.

18. Barbara Kingsolver, *Holding the Line, Women in the Great Arizona Mine Strike of 1983* (Ithaca: ILR Press, 1989), pp. 1–12.

19. Quoted in Kingsolver, p. 2.

20. Quoted in Kingsolver, p. 10.

21. *See* Ruiz *in* del Castillo.

22. For details on the Bracero Program, *see* Acuña, pp. 261–266; Cockcroft, *Outlaws,* pp. 67–92.

23. For more on the causes of these clubs, now called gangs, *see* James Diego Vigil, *Barrio Gangs* (Austin: University of Texas Press, 1988), pp. 24–43.

24. For details on Sleepy Lagoon and the zoot-suit

riots, *see* Acuña, pp. 324–329; García, pp. 171–173; Cockcroft, *Outlaws,* pp. 62–63. On why Fierro de Bright had to leave, see below.

25. Mick Martin and Marsha Porter, *Video Movie Guide 1992* (New York: Ballantine Books, 1991), p. 86.

26. On McCarran-Walter, *see* Cockcroft, *Outlaws,* pp. 73–74, 213–214. For the cold war and the witch-hunt, *see* Victor S. Navasky, *Naming Names* (New York: Viking Press, 1980), pp. 20–44; Don E. Carleton, *Red Scare! Right-Wing Hysteria, Fifties Fanaticism and Their Legacy in Texas* (Austin: Texas Monthly Press, 1985); and David Caute, *The Great Fear* (New York: Simon and Schuster, 1978).

27. For details, *see* García, pp. 167–173.

28. Quoted in Ruiz, *in* Del Castillo, p. 293.

29. For more details, *see* Acuña, pp. 253 and 283–293; Cockcroft, *Hispanics;* García, pp. 19, 101–103; Telgen and Kamp, p. 212.

30. For more on ANMA and Mine-Mill, *see* Acuña, pp. 234, 278–279; and García, pp. 199–227. On the Empire Zinc strike and how *Salt of the Earth* was made, *see* Cockcroft, *Outlaws,* pp. 74–75.

31. *See* Cockcroft, *Outlaws,* pp. 78–79.

Four

1. For more information on this period, *see* Felix M. Padilla, *Puerto Rican Chicago* (Notre Dame, Indiana: University of Notre Dame Press, 1987), pp. 23–28.

2. Quoted in James D. Cockcroft, *Neighbors in Turmoil: Latin America* (New York: Harper & Row, 1989), p. 252 (revised ed., Chicago: Nelson Hall, 1995).

3. For details, see Cockcroft, pp. 250–254, 278–280.

4. Quoted in Cockcroft, p. 280.

5. For more details, *see* Padilla, pp. 40–41.

6. For more on Capetillo, *see* Diana Telgen and Jim Kamp, eds., *Notable Hispanic American Women* (Detroit: Gale Research Inc., 1993), p. 72.

7. Quoted in Virginia E. Sánchez Korrol, *From Colonia to Community* (Westport: Greenwood Press, 1983), p. 4.

8. Details on this long-hidden period can be found in the pioneering work of Sánchez Korrol, pp. 11–47. *See also* Kal Wagenheim and Olga Jiménez de Wagenheim, *The Puerto Ricans* (New York: Praeger, 1973), pp. 229–236.

9. Wagenheim and Jiménez de Wagenheim, pp. 229, 236.

10. The 1925 census listed less than 3 percent of the 7,322 counted Hispanic individuals in New York City as professionals.

11. For details, *see* Sánchez Korrol, pp. 65–68 and 112–114.

12. Padilla, p. 31.

13. Quoted in Sánchez Korrol, p. 45.

14. Quoted from the *New York Times*, Feb. 4, 1928, in Wagenheim and Jiménez de Wagenheim, p. 52.

15. Quoted in Wagenheim and Jiménez de Wagenheim, p. 152.

16. Quoted in Wagenheim and Jiménez de Wagenheim, p. 154.

17. Quoted in Sánchez Korrol, pp. 103–104.

18. For more on the early politics of the barrio, *see* Sánchez Korrol, pp. 183–187.

19. For more on religion, *see* Nicolás Kanellos, ed., *The Hispanic-American Almanac* (Detroit: Gale Research Inc., 1993), pp. 378–386.

20. Judith Ortiz Cofer, "Latin Women Pray" in *Triple Crown* (Tempe: Bilingual Press, 1987), p. 89.

21. Adalberto Gilberto López and James Petras, eds., *Puerto Rico and Puerto Ricans: Studies in History and Society* (Cambridge, Mass.: Schenkman Publishing Co., 1974), pp. 327–328; and Sánchez Korrol, pp. 75–76, 156.

22. *See* James D. Cockcroft, *Hispanics in the Struggle for Social Justice* (New York: Franklin Watts, 1994).

23. Sánchez Korrol, p. 197.

24. For more, *see* Cockcroft, *Neighbors,* pp. 275–293.

25. See Edna Acosta-Belén, *The Puerto Rican Woman* (New York: Praeger, 1986), p. 14.

26. For a vivid description of such a journey, *see* the excerpt from Dan Wakefield's *Island in the City, in* Wagenheim and Jiménez de Wagenheim, pp. 234–239.

27. Quoted in Wagenheim and Jiménez de Wagenheim, p. 241.

28. Quoted in Wagenheim and Jiménez de Wagenheim, pp. 233–234.

29. Angela Jorge, "The Black Puerto Rican Woman in Contemporary American Society," *in* Acosta-Belén, pp. 134–141.

30. Quoted in Gerald Meyer, *Vito Marcantonio: Radical Politician 1902–1954* (Albany: State University of New York Press, 1989), p. 183.

31. For more, *see* Meyer, pp. 144–172.

32. *See also* Telgen and Kamp, pp. 310–312.

33. Adalberto Gilberto López, "The Puerto Rican Diaspora: A Survey" *in* López and Petras, p. 326.

Five

1. Kal Wagenheim and Olga Jiménez de Wagenheim, *The Puerto Ricans* (New York: Praeger, 1973), pp. 258–263.

2. Quoted in Francesco Cordasco and Eugene Bucchioni, eds., *The Puerto Rican Experience* (Totowa, New Jersey: Rowman and Littlefield, 1973), p. 256.

3. Author's interviews, 1962–1963.

4. Quoted in Thomas Howard Tarantino and Rev. Dismas Becker, eds., *Welfare Mothers Speak Out: We Ain't Gonna Shuffle Anymore* (New York: W.W. Norton & Co., Inc., 1972), p. 64.

5. Quoted in Tarantino and Becker, p. 66. For Mrs. Castro's full commentary, *see* pp. 66–71.

6. For more on the Berkeley free speech movement

and Joan Baez, *see* Hedda Garza, *Joan Baez* (New York: Chelsea House, 1991), pp. 15–29.

7. Quoted in Alfredo Mirandé and Evangelina Enríquez, *La Chicana: The Mexican-American Woman* (Chicago: University of Chicago Press, 1979), p. 233.

8. Quoted in Diana Telgen and Jim Kamp, eds., *Notable Hispanic American Women* (Detroit: Gale Research Inc., 1993), p. 211.

9. Quoted in Rosalyn Baxandall, Linda Gordon, and Susan Reverby, eds., *America's Working Women* (New York: Random House, 1976), p. 365.

10. Quoted in Baxandall, Gordon, and Reverby, p. 367.

11. Quoted in Mirandé and Enríquez, p. 241.

12. For more details on the treatment of women in the 1960s movements, *see* Mirandé and Enríquez, pp. 202–243.

13. Quoted in Baxandall, Gordon, and Reverby, pp. 366–367.

14. Quoted in Baxandall, Gordon, and Reverby, p. 371.

15. For more on the Chicago Young Lords, *see* Frank Browning, "From Rumble to Revolution: the Young Lords," in Cordasco and Bucchioni, pp. 231–245; Felix M. Padilla, *Puerto Rican Chicago* (Notre Dame, Indiana: University of Notre Dame Press, 1987), pp. 126–137; Wagenheim and Jiménez de Wagenheim, p. 236.

16. Quoted in Padilla, p. 121.

17. See Rodolfo Acuña, *Occupied America: A History of Chicanos* (New York: HarperCollins 1988), ix.

18. For a biography of Rodolfo Gonzalez, *see* Nicolás Kanellos, ed., *The Hispanic-American Almanac* (Detroit: Gale Research Inc., 1993), p. 380.

19. For more on the Crusade for Justice and the Chicano movement in general, *see* Carlos Muñoz, Jr., *Youth, Identity, Power* (New York: Verso, 1989), pp. 50–64.

20. Quoted in Joan Moore and Harry Pachon, *His-*

panics in the United States (Englewood Cliffs, New Jersey: Prentice-Hall, Inc., 1985), p. 182.

21. For details on this victory, *see* John Staples Shockley, *Chicano Revolt in a Texas Town* (Notre Dame: University of Notre Dame Press, 1974).

22. For more details, *see* James D. Cockcroft, *Latinos in the Struggle for Social Justice* (New York: Franklin Watts, 1994).

23. For details on the Vietnam War and the antiwar movement, *see* Howard Zinn, *A People's History of the United States* (New York: HarperPerennial, 1980), pp. 461–492.

24. *See* Gilberto López y Rivas, *The Chicanos* (New York: Monthly Review Press, 1973), pp. 168–174.

25. Quoted in Sonia A. López, "The Role of the Chicana within the Student Movement" in Rosaura Sánchez and Rosa Martinez Cruz, *Essays on La Mujer* (Los Angeles: Chicano Studies Center Publication, UCLA, 1977), p. 21.

26. The full statement appears in López y Rivas, pp. 171–174.

27. For details on the history of the Young Lords Party, *see* Cordasco and Bucchioni, pp. 246–275.

28. Quoted in Cordasco and Bucchioni, p. 246. Recently, there has been further investigation of the treatment of women in the Young Lords Party. Isa M. Infante's dissertation on "Politization of Immigrant Women from Puerto Rico and the Dominican Republic" (University of California, 1977) discusses the sexist treatment of women by Hispanic male radical community leaders and includes those within the Young Lords Party.

29. Quoted in Baxandall, Gordon, and Reverby, pp. 371–372.

30. Mari Jo Buhle, Paul Buhle, and Dan Georgakas, eds., *Encyclopedia of the American Left* (New York: Garland Publishing, Inc., 1990), pp. 834–841.

31. Quoted in Cordasco and Bucchioni, p. 251.

32. *See* López y Rivas, pp. 162–167.

33. For further details, *see* Acuña, pp. 346–350.

34. For more, *see* Acuña, pp. 342–344, 350–352; Padilla, pp. 165–179, 250; Zinn, pp. 453, 455.

35. Pablo "Yoruba" Guzmán, "Puerto Rican Barrio Politics in the United States," *in* Clara E. Rodríguez, Virginia Sánchez Korrol, and José Oscar Alers, eds., *The Puerto Rican Struggle: Essays on Survival in the U.S.* (Maplewood: The Waterfront Press, 1980), pp. 127–128.

36. Richard Griswold del Castillo, *The Treaty of Guadalupe Hidalgo: A Legacy of Conflict* (Norman: University of Oklahoma Press, 1990), p. 144.

37. Marta Cotera, "Feminism: The Chicana and the Anglo Versions," in Margarita B. Melville, ed., *Twice a Minority: Mexican American Women* (St. Louis: C.V. Mosby, Inc., 1980), p. 227.

38. Quoted in Mirandé and Enríquez, p. 243.

39. For a review of of the Chicana movement from 1960 through 1970, *see* Melville, pp. 228–234.

40. Edna Acosta-Belén, *The Puerto Rican Woman* (New York: Praeger, 1979), pp. 131–133. For more on this issue, consult Iris Lopéz, "Social Coercion and Sterilization among Puerto Rican Women," 8, 3 (1983), pp. 27–40.

41. *See* Gena Corea, *The Hidden Malpractice* (New York: Harper & Row, 1977), pp. 140–144.

42. Quoted in Carlos G. Velez-I., "The Nonconsenting Sterilization of Mexican Women in Los Angeles" in Melville, p. 245.

43. For details on the attitudes of Chicanas toward abortion, *see* Maria Luisa Urdaneta, "Chicana Use of Abortion," in Melville, pp. 33–51.

44. *See* Muñoz, pp. 75–98.

45. Quoted in Muñoz, p. 117.

46. For details, *see* Padilla, pp. 214–221.

47. *See* Padilla, pp. 165–179, 250.

48. *See* Adalberto Gilberto López and James Petras,

Puerto Rico and Puerto Ricans (Cambridge, Mass.: Schenkman Publishing Co., 1974), pp. 331–334.

Six

1. *See* Hedda Garza, *Women in Medicine* (New York: Franklin Watts, 1994).

2. In 1970, parity for Latinos in most professions did not even reach 20 percent! For parity tables *see* U.S. Department of Health and Human Services, *Minorities and Women in the Health Fields* (Washington, D.C.: GPO, 1990). The term "parity" is often used to indicate the percentage of people of a particular ethnic or racial group compared with their percentage in the population. One hundred percent parity represents full participation.

3. For background and details *see* Nicolás Kanellos, ed., *The Hispanic-American Almanac* (Detroit: Gale Research Inc., 1993), p. 356.

4. Data is from *Chronicle of Higher Education,* March 18, 1992, p. A-35.

5. Parity of 50 percent had not even been attained. Male Latino physicians, for example, numbered 22,978 in 1990, but there were only 5,803 Latina doctors, out of a total of 465,468 male and 121,247 female physicians nationally. In other health professions such as dentistry, even lower parity scores were achieved. Other professions reflect similar or worse imbalances. Rounding off the numbers, of over 747,000 lawyers, about 18,000 are Latino, males outnumbering females by a 2 to 1 margin. In other professions and job categories, the ratios are even worse. These figures are taken from the latest EEOC Census/ Equal Employment Opportunity Special File on computer tape, scheduled for publication in 1992.

6. Parity for Hispanics in medicine rose to 78 percent by 1979–1980, but then declined again to 64 percent ten years later! *See* U.S. Department of Health and Human Services, 1990.

7. On the other hand, almost one-fourth of lower-status and lower-paid practical nurses were members of minority groups in 1985–1986. *See* U.S. Department of Health and Human Services, 1990, pp. 17, 42, 85. Of first year total enrollment in medical school, in recent years out of 16,868, 4,335 were minority students, including 295 Mexican Americans, 127 Puerto Ricans, and 288 other Hispanics—a very low percentage indeed. Of these Latino groups, a mere 120, 59, and 103 were women. Black women were more than half the total of enrollees, and Asians were far above parity and no longer considered an underrepresented minority. For women in general, out of 81,410 physicians in residency programs in 1987–88, females were 27.8 percent. Dentistry has only recently opened up for women.

8. According to EEOC data, the percentages of Latinos range from 1.6 to a high of 3.5 in these fields, with almost no women. By the early 1990s there were well over half a million attorneys in the United States. Of those, 12,330 were Hispanic males and 6,282 Hispanic females.

9. For details on Latina attorneys, *see* Kanellos, pp. 238–241.

10. Quoted in Diana Telgen and Jim Kamp, eds., *Notable Hispanic American Women* (Detroit: Gale Research Inc., 1993), p. 197. Unless otherwise stated, all subsequent biographical sketches and quotations from individual Latinas may be located in alphabetical order in Telgen and Kamp.

11. *New York Times,* Dec. 2, 1993.

12. *New York Times,* Dec. 2, 1993.

13. Harry Pachon and Louis DeSipio, "Latino Elected Officials in the 1990s," *PS: Political Science and Politics,* June 1992, p. 213.

14. New York City Department of Health AIDS Surveillance Update, Sept, 27, 1989.

15. The coalition is located at 315 Wyckoff Ave.,

Brooklyn, N.Y. 11237. At present, Julia Andino is working with mothers who have AIDS.

16. The total number of postsecondary teachers in 1990 was 615,068, of whom 214,046 were women. Latino males held 11,623 posts and Latinas 9,094, once again less than 5 percent of the total for both sexes (EEOC census data).

17. Soon to be published by Temple University Press is an anthology edited by Altagracia Ortiz, *Puerto Rican Women Workers in the Twentieth Century.* Ortiz is currently writing a history of Puerto Rican women workers in the United States and Puerto Rico.

18. Margarita Gomez, "A Place at the Table," in *Hispanic,* October 1992, p. 16.

19. *Hispanic,* October 1992, p. 60.

20. Quoted in "Top 25 places for Hispanics to Work in the Federal Government," *in Hispanic,* April 1992, p. 28.

21. U.S. Bureau of the Census, 1987 Survey of Minority-Owned Businesses, *Census and You* (Washington, D.C.: GPO), August 1991, p. 10.

22. For more on Lation theater, *see* Kanellos, pp. 505–541.

23. For more on Latino filmmakers, actors, etc., *see* Kanellos, pp. 573–583.

24. EEOC census-based data.

25. For more on Rivera and his legacy, *see* James D. Cockcroft, *Diego Rivera* (New York: Chelsea House, 1991).

26. For details on the subject of Latinos in music, *see* Kanellos, pp. 595–619.

27. Also known as *Bizet's Carmen,* the film was made by a joint French-Italian production company and is available on video.

28. Author's interview with Lares, July, 1991.

29. For more on U.S. policy in Chile, *see* Hedda Garza, *Salvador Allende* (New York: Chelsea House,

1989). On the Dominicans, *see* James D. Cockcroft, *Neighbors in Turmoil: Latin America* (New York: Harper & Row, 1989, revised ed., Nelson-Hall, 1994), pp. 294–310; Sherri Grasmuck and Patricia R. Pessar, *Between Two Islands* (Berkeley: University of California Press, 1991), pp. 98–208.

30. For more on the Cubans, *see* Revecca Morales and Frank Bonilla, eds., *Latinos in a Changing U.S. Economy* (Newbury Park: Sage, 1993), pp. 121–122; Barbara Grenquist, *Cubans* (New York: Franklin Watts, 1991), p. 45.

31. For more, *see* James D. Cockcroft, *Outlaws in the Promised Land* (New York: Grove, 1988), pp. 173, 242–252.

32. The author of a major textbook on Latin America described it as a "long dark night" of "state terrorism"—Cockcroft, *Neighbors*, 3.

33. For more on the Domincans, *see* James Ferguson. *The Dominican Republic Beyond the Lighthouse* (London: The Latin American Bureau, 1992), pp. 76–78; Nancy Foner, ed., *New Immigrants in New York* (New York: Columbia University Press, 1987), pp. 104–126.

34. The 15-minute 1986 color video is availbable from the UFW, La Paz, California.

35. In 1993, Cesar Chavez died at age 66 before he could see the completion of the antipesticide campaign, which continues today.

36. For details, see Frank D. Bean, Barry Edmonston and Jeffrey S. Passel, *Undocumented Immigration to the United States* (Washington, D.C.: The Urban Institute Press, 1990), pp. 222–225; and Cockcroft, *Outlaws*, pp. 115–151, 209–238, 283.

37. For details, *see* Cockcroft, *Outlaws*, pp. 175–208.

38. Quoted in Barbara Kingsolver, *Holding the Line: Women in the Great Arizona Mine Strike Of 1983* (Ithaca: ILR Press, Cornell University, 1989), p. 135.

39. Quoted in *Guardian*, June 13, 1990, p. 19.

40. Quoted in Kingsolver, p. 61.

41. Kanellos, p. 334.

42. For details, *see* Sam Roberts, "A New Face for American Labor," *New York Times Magazine*, May 10, 1992, p. 14.

43. For background and details, *see* the pioneering work of Cockcroft, *Outlaws*, pp. 39, 209–259.

44. In 1993, for example, Latina "illegals" joining a union at Long Island City's S.T.C. Knitwear were reported to the INS (*New York Times*, June 15, 1993).

45. *New York Times*, April 29, 1990; Cockcroft, *Outlaws*, p. 255; "ABC Prime Time television segment," Dec. 2, 1993.

46. The shrinking job market was the main cause of the spreading xenophobia according to a research report to the Ford Foundation by Robert L. Bach and others— *Changing Relations* (New York: Ford Foundation, 1993).

47. *Diálogo* (Newsletter of National Puerto Rican Policy Network, Summer 1993), pp. 11–12; Kanellos, p. 350; *New York Times*, September 4 and 15, 1988, March 23, 1989, Oct. 7, 1993; U.S. Bureau of the Census, *Current Population Reports*, P20–455, p.8.

48. For more on gangs, *see* Mary G. Harris, *Cholas: Latino Girls and Gangs* (New York: AMS Press, 1988), p. 80ff; James Diego Vigil, *Barrio Gangs* (Austin: University of Texas Press, 1988), pp. 16–34.

49. For details, *see* the individual city chapters in Morales and Bonilla.

50. For more on this pattern, *see* Susan Faludi, *Backlash* (New York: Crown Publishers, Inc., 1991); Edwin Melendez, Clara Rodriguez and Janis Barry Figueroa, eds., *Hispanics in the Labor Force* (New York: Plenum Press, 1991), pp. 6–20; Morales and Bonilla, pp. 1–36, 91.

Bibliography

* Books especially recommended for students.

Achor, Shirley. *Mexican Americans in a Dallas Barrio.* Tucson: University of Arizona Press, 1978.

Acosta-Belén, Edna and Barbara R. Sjostrom, eds. *The Hispanic Experience in the United States.* New York: Praeger Publishers, 1988.

Acosta-Belén, Edna. *The Puerto Rican Woman.* New York: Praeger Publishers, 1986.

*Acuña, Rodolfo. *Occupied America: A History of Chicanos.* New York: HarperCollins Publishers, 1988.

Baxandall, Rosalyn, Linda Gordon and Susan Reverby. *America's Working Women.* New York: Random House, 1976.

Boswell, Thomas D. and James R. Curtis. *The Cuban-American Experience.* Totowa, New Jersey: Rowman & Allanheld Publishers, 1984.

*Cockcroft, James D. *Hispanics in the Struggle for Social Justice.* New York: Franklin Watts, 1994.

*Cockcroft, James D. *Outlaws in the Promised Land.* New York: Grove Press, Inc., 1986.

Cordasco, Francesco and Eugene Bucchioni, eds. *The Puerto Rican Experience.* Totowa, New Jersey: Rowman and Littlefield, 1973.

*Corea, Gena. *The Hidden Malpractice.* New York: Harper & Row Publishers, 1977.

*Crittenden, Ann. *Sanctuary.* New York: Weidenfeld & Nicolson, 1988.

Del Castillo, Adelaida, ed. *Between Borders: Essays on Mexicana/Chicana History.* Encino: Floricanto Press, 1990.

Faludi, Susan. *Backlash.* New York: Crown Publishers, Inc., 1991.

Ferguson, James. *The Dominican Republic Beyond the Lighthouse.* London: The Latin American Bureau, 1992.

Foner, Nancy, ed. *New Immigrants in New York.* New York: Columbia University Press, 1987.

Garcá, Mario T. *Mexican Americans.* New Haven: Yale University Press, 1989.

*Garza, Hedda. *Joan Baez.* New York: Chelsea House, 1991.

*Grenquist, Barbara. *Cubans.* New York: Franklin Watts, 1991.

*Hadley-Garcia, George. *Hispanic Hollywood.* New York: Citadel Press, 1990.

Harris, Mary G. *Cholas: Latino Girls and Gangs.* New York: AMS Press, 1988.

*Kanellos, Nicolś, ed., *The Hispanic-American Almanac.* Detroit: Gale Research Inc., 1993.

*Kingsolver, Barbara. *Holding the Line: Women in the Great Arizona Mine Strike of 1983.* New York: ILR Press, Cornell University, 1989.

López y Rivas, Gilberto. *The Chicanos.* New York: Monthly Review Press, 1973.

*Melville, Margarita B., ed. *Twice A Minority: Mexican American Women.* St. Louis: C.V. Mosby Co., 1980.

*Meyers, Gerald. *Vito Marcantonio.* Albany: State University of New York Press, 1989.

Mirandé, Alfredo and Evangelina Enréquez. *La Chicana:*

The Mexican-American Woman. Chicago: University of Chicago Press, 1979.

Muñoz, Jr., Carlos. *Youth, Identity, Power*. New York: Verso, 1989.

*Padilla, Felix M. *Puerto Rican Chicago*. Notre Dame, Indiana: University of Notre Dame Press, 1987.

Prohias, Rafael J. and Lourdes Casal. *The Cuban Minority in the U.S.*, vol 1. New York: Arno Press, 1980.

Rendon, Armando B. *Chicano Manifesto*. New York: The Macmillan Company, 1971.

Rodríguez, Clara E. *Puerto Ricans Born in the U.S.A.* Boston: Unwin Hyman, Inc., 1989.

*Sánchez Korrol, Virgina E. *From Colonia to Community*. Westport: Greenwood Press, 1983.

*Telgen, Diana and Jim Kamp, eds. *Notable Hispanic American Women*. Detroit: Gale Research Inc., 1993.

*Wagenheim, Kal and Olga Jimenez de Wagenheim, *The Puerto Ricans*. New York: Praeger Publishers, 1973.

*Zinn, Howard. *A People's History of the United States*. New York: HarperCollins Publishers, 1990.

Magazines and Documents

Hispanic, published by Hispanic Publishing Corp., 111 Massachusetts Ave., NW, Suite 410, Washington D.C. 20001.

U.S. Bureau of the Census. *Current Population Reports*, P23-183, "Hispanic Americans Today." Washington, D,C.: GPO, 1993.

U.S. Department of Health & Human Services. "Minorities and Women in the Health Fields," 1990.

Index

Casal, Lourdes, 153–154
Casals, Rosemary, 142
Castro, Clementina, 110
Catholic church, and Hispanics, 30–31, 40, 96–97
Central Americans, 154–155
Chavez, Cesar, 106, 111, 113, 117, 122, 155
Chavez Fernandez, Alicia, 112
Chicago, Illinois, Hispanics in, 33, 34–37, 58–59, 65–66, 83, 129. See also Young Lords
Chicana Service Action Center, 127
Chicanas: in labor movement, 65, 67–71; and Puerto Ricans, 82; sterilization of, 128. See also Mexican American women
Chicano documentary cinema, 146
Chicano Moratorium, 125
Chicano movement, 117–118, 119, 120–121, 126, 136, 158
Chicano studies, 139
Chicano theater movement, 144
Chileans, 153
Chinese Exclusion Act (1882), 28
Cisneros, Sandra, 148
Civil Rights Act (1964), 107, 129, 131
Civil rights movement, 105, 146; and COINTELPRO, 125–126; Latinos and, 71–72, 106–107, 116, 133
Clinton, Bill, 136
Coalition for Hispanic Family Services, 137
Cofer, Judith Ortiz, 96–97
COINTELPRO, 125–126
Cold war, 77–80, 102–103
College students, Latino, 116, 132–133

College and university teachers, Latino, 139–140
Colmennares, Margarita H., 140
Colón, Miriam, 143
Comisión Femenil Mexicana, 127, 128, 136
Community Service Organization (CSO), 80
Compadrazgo, 93
Composers, Latino, 150
Congreso, El, 72–73, 81
Congress of Industrial Organizations (CIO), 63–64, 79–80
Coolidge, Calvin, 91–92
Corea, Chick, 149
Cortina, Juan "Cheno," 28
Cotera, Marta, 126–127
Council for the Protection of Minority Rights, 73, 75
Crusade for Justice, 117, 119
Cruz, Celia, 150
Cuba, history of, 84, 85, 88, 151, 152–153, 154
Cubans, 83, 85, 143, 152–154

Daley, Richard M., 115, 136
de León, Candido, 130
de Soto, Rosana, 147
del Castillo, Adelaida, 127, 139
Del Rio, Dolores, 72
Delgado, Diane, 157
Diamond Walnut strike, 157
Díaz, Porfirio, 37–38, 40–41, 44–45
Domingo, Placido, 152
Dominicans, 153, 155
Drug, Hospital and Health Care Employees Union, District 1199, 158–159
Durazo, María Elena, 158

McCarthyism. *See* Witch-hunt
Machismo, 14–16, 44, 122
Malvaéz, Inés, 44
Managerial employment, 141
Manifest Destiny, 22, 86
Marcantonio, Vito, 95, 97–98, 102–103
"Marielitos," 153
Marshall, Lupe, 65
Martí, José, 85
Martika, 151
Martinez, Elizabeth, 116
Medical experimentation issue, 127–128
Melville, Margarita B., 139
Mendoza, Cirilo, 44
Mexican American Legal Defense Fund (MALDEF), 134, 135, 162
Mexican-American War (1848), 24–26, 46
Mexican American Youth Organization (MAYO), 118
Mexican Americans: and "Brown Scare," 51–52; employment of, 55; and First Mexican Congress, 51; and LULAC, 56–57; and Johnson administration, 116–117; serving in World War II, 75, 76. *See also* Chicano movement
Mexican immigrants: and agricultural labor, 50–51; attitude toward Mexico, 37–39; and Bracero Program, 75–76; deportation during "Operation Wetback," 81; and Mexican Revolution, 48; and nativism, 159–160; and "revolving door," 51; during World War I, 53–54. *See also* "Undocumented" immigrant workers

Mexican Liberal Party. *See* PLM
Mexican miners, 39–46, 48–50, 52, 74–75
Mexican Revolution, 44–45, 47–48
Mexican theater companies, 143
Mexican and Mexican American women: and American feminism, 46; during California gold rush, 26–27; in early Southwest, 17–33, 42; family heads, 32; PLM leaders, 44–45, 47; as wage workers, 32, 65, 67, 69–71
Mexico, history, 22–26. *See also* Mexican-American War
Migenes-Johnson, Julia, 152
Milan, Myrna, 135
Mine-Mill, 80–82
Mohr, Nicholasa, 147
Molina, Gloria, 136
Morales, Sylvia, 146
Moreno, Luisa, 68, 70–72, 73, 75, 79–80, 81
Moreno, Rita, 145–146
Mount, Julia Luna, 80
Movimiento Estudiantil Chicano de Aztlan, El (MECHA), 120, 128
Muñoz Marin, Luis, 92, 99, 100, 101
Muralists, 148–149
Musicians, 149–151
Mutual aid societies, 41–42, 56, 88

National American Woman Suffrage Association (NAWSA), 46–47
National Association for Puerto Rican Civil Rights, 135

81, 88, 100–101; political involvement, 94–95, 97–99; professionals in 1920s, 89; and racism, 101–102; sterilization of, 100; as U.S. citizens, 54, 90, 99. *See also* Spanish Harlem
Puerto Rico: history, 83–87, 91–92, 95–96, 98–100; birth control pill tests in, 127–128; film industry, 146

Quezada, Leticia, 138–139
Quinn, Anthony, 72

Racism, Latinos and, 13–14, 26–30, 31, 137; and Bracero Program, 75–76; and "Brown Scare," 51–52; and Chicana feminism,120–121; and conquest of Texas, 23; and economic gap among Latinos, 162; and intelligence test issue, 97–98; and Mexican women, 60; in mining towns, 39–40; and Puerto Ricans, 92–93, 101–102; and Raza Unida party, 118; and zoot-suit riots, 76–77
Ramírez, Sara Estela, 45
Ramirez, Tina, 152
Rape, 18–19, 29, 30, 31
Raza Unida party, La, 118, 128
Red-baiting, 61, 64–65, 68, 99. *See also* Witch-hunt
"Revolving door," 51, 56
Ríos, Carlos, 105
Riots, 115, 118–119
Rivera, Chita, 147
Rivera, Dennis, 158–159
Rivera, Diego, 148
Rockefeller, John D., 48, 49

Rodriguez, Celia, 80
Rodriguez, Dr. Helen, 124, 137
Rodriguez, Lina S., 135
Rodriguez, Patricia, 149
Rodriguez, Tito, 150
Roldan, Julio, 125
Roma, Rosa, 90–91
Roman, Fina, 157
Ronstadt, Linda, 150–151
Roosevelt, Eleanor, 105
Roosevelt, Franklin Delano, 61, 64, 77, 95
Ros-Lehtinen, Ileana, 136

Sager, Manuela Solis, 68
Salazar, Rubén, 125
Salcido, Abraham, 41–42, 43
Salsa, 150
Salt War (1877), 29
Salvadorans, 154
Salzman-Webb, Marilyn, 114
Sanchez Korrol, Virginia, 139
Sánchez, Maria E., 138
Sanctuary Movement, 154
Sanger, Margaret, 59
Santa Anna, General, 23
Santana, Carlos, 149, 151
Santeria, 96
Santiago, Isaura, 140
Santos, Miriam, 136
Scapegoating, of Mexican immigrants, 38–39, 48
Scientists and engineers, 140
Segregation, 39, 55–56, 71–72
Serafina L., 108–109
Sexism: and Latinas, 13–14; and SDS, 113–114
Sheila E., 151
Silva de Cintrón, Josefina, 98
"Sit-down" strikes, 64
Slavery, 22, 23, 84–85